insight text guide

Sue Tweg

Medea

Euripides

insight

▶innovative ▶engaging ▶evolving

First published in 1999, based on the translation by Philip Vellacott.
Reprinted with corrections in 2009.
Revised and reprinted in 2014 with text revisions based on the translation by John Davie. Reprinted in 2015, 2016, 2017 (twice), 2019, 2020, 2021, 2024, 2025.

Insight Publications Pty Ltd
3/350 Charman Road
Cheltenham VIC 3192
Australia
Tel: +61 3 8571 4950
Email: books@insightpublications.com.au

www.insightpublications.com.au

National Library of Australia Cataloguing-in-Publication entry:

Tweg, Sue.
Insight text guide: Euripides' Medea.
Bibliography
9781875882274
1. Euripides, 480–406 BC Medea. 2. Euripides, 480–406 BC Criticism and interpretation. I. Title. (Series: Insight text guide)

Other ISBNs:
9781925175677 (digital)

Cover design: The Modern Art Production Group

Printed by Markono Print Media Pte Ltd

contents

CHARACTER MAP

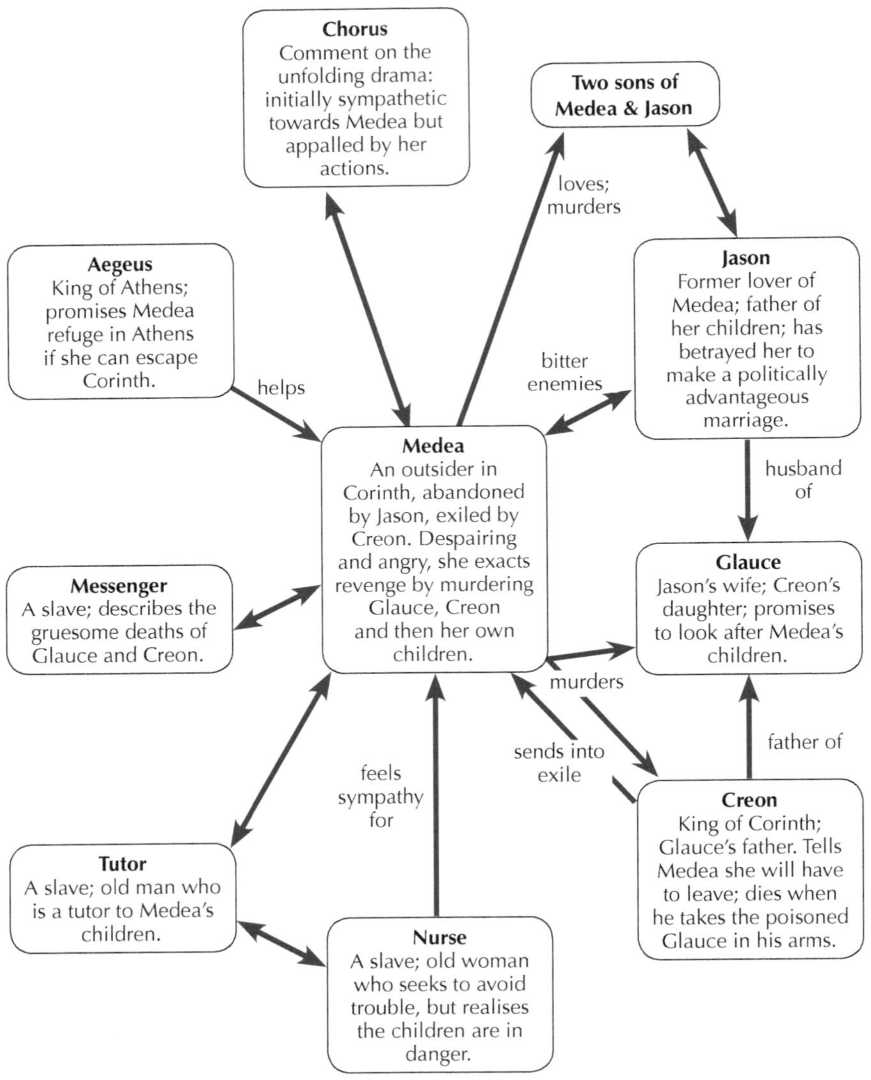

INTRODUCTION

Medea was first performed over two thousand years ago. It's one of a very select group of plays – thirty-one in all (with several hundred others lost) – that still speak across the centuries from fifth century BC Greece. Nineteen of all the plays that remain are by Euripides. Euripides' version of *Medea* was the first, and is the only surviving, play out of seven on the same subject by other writers.

The underlying theme of this play is deadly conflict, somehow appropriate since *Medea* was first performed in 431 BC, the year hostilities broke out between the rival city states of Athens and Sparta. This was the beginning of the Peloponnesian War that would drag on for the rest of Euripides' life. He died about three years before peace was concluded, with the defeat of Athens in 404 BC. Little is known about his life, although there is one poignant connection with the subject matter of *Medea*: for some reason, when he was over seventy, Euripides left Athens for voluntary self-exile in Macedonia, where he wrote his last great play *The Bacchae*.

Throughout its long performance history, *Medea* has moved audiences to pity and terror, the supreme tragic emotions according to Aristotle. Medea herself is one of the great roles for an actor, demanding psychological strength, intense emotion and nuance.

During the Middle Ages and Renaissance, Medea's cruelty in killing her children became a main focus of interest. Shakespeare connected Jason and Medea as tragic lovers in *The Merchant of Venice*, also identifying her as a sorceress, which was a favourite way of representing her in Pre-Raphaelite art. With her magic cauldron, she becomes the beautiful, cunning witch, sexually alluring but deadly.

Medea did not win the first prize for Euripides in the 431 BC festival, probably because it spoke out too plainly to Athenian citizens about men's relationships with women, passion set against reason, and a 'civilised' city's rough treatment of aliens. The play also criticised a popular hero, and contained an ambiguous characterisation, bordering on the disrespectful, of Aegeus, the wily but sterile old king of Athens. Euripides was never a popular playwright in Athens: *Medea*, his first real tragedy, gives us some idea why.

BACKGROUND & CONTEXT

Greece in Euripides' time

Ancient Greece, and Athens especially under the rule of Pericles from the mid-fifth century BC, is still popularly thought of as the home of democracy and the model of 'civilised' life, a place where philosophers like Socrates and Plato could think and teach, where sciences and the arts could flourish. This romantic view of Athens as the ideal of civilised community life was absorbed into Roman culture, later filtered through the Middle Ages into Renaissance Europe and thence, through literature, mythology and art, into our world, which is where we begin to study *Medea*. If Athenian life in reality was less than glorious, we get hints about it through the work of Euripides.

Athenian democracy and citizenship

Medea is 'Athenocentric', conscious that it is playing to a crowd largely made up of Athenian citizens, who identify with every reference to their democratic state. At the heart of Greek tragedy as an art form is a concern about Athens and what it stands for: explicit criticism is rare, although, as we'll see in *Medea*, citizens at a play were often challenged to think about ingrained attitudes and assumptions.

Euripides, a citizen of democratic Athens, had certain rights and responsibilities. Since early in the fifth century BC, Attica, a geographical unit of ten 'tribes' under the control of the most powerful city, Athens, was subdivided into townships or suburbs called 'demes'. This is the origin of the word 'democracy': all citizens, rich and poor, were expected to play a part in the maintenance of their state and to demonstrate interest in what was going on through public debate of matters concerning Attica.

Of course, not everyone qualified to be a citizen, which is why it is praised in drama as something special, to be valued as a privilege.

The greatest disaster that could befall a citizen was the loss of that identity. *Medea* is all about the trauma of exile and lost identity which Athens steps in to restore. One of the Choric odes specifically focuses on Athens as the epitome of harmonious civil life, blessed by the gods. In another play, by Sophocles, a character in exile declares that being without a 'polis' (city) is equivalent to being dead.

Aristotle, writing a century after Euripides, defined a citizen as male, adult, freeborn, legitimate, of citizen descent on both the mother's and father's sides, and with an active share in public decision-taking and office-holding. In Euripides' time this meant about thirty thousand adult men in Athens, all of whom were expected to take some interest in state religious festival activities.

Theatre as a public educator

Greek dramatic spectacles were more than entertainment. They were acts of religion, involving the population as an ongoing public duty. Tragic theatre characteristically both confirmed and questioned Athenian democracy because it was political theatre, staged for and by the 'polis' of Athens. One of the aims of Greek tragedy was to educate citizens in the practice of good citizenship: 'Look, this is how we do things'; 'Listen, this is how to argue and make a debate'. The ideal to be achieved in personal life was moderation, 'Nothing in excess'. Plays like *Medea* articulated difficulties experienced by human beings trying to understand fundamental questions of duty and justice in situations of conflict, where the gods could be appealed to, but rarely gave direct guidance.

The gods

You can find many studies arguing about how Greek tragic playwrights introduced the gods into their plots and what they believed. Despite disagreement among experts, there's no doubt that Greek tragedies were deeply concerned with spiritual things, exploring just how Zeus and his pantheon of gods on Mount Olympus interfered in human concerns. How far were mortals free to pursue or avoid disasters of their own making, within a cosmos that also had room for concepts of Fate, Right (Themis) and a complex Revenge/Justice/Punishment idea (in Greek – Dike)? Hall argues that: 'A crucial frontier defined by tragedy is that between man and god' (cited in Easterling 1997, p.96). It is suggested that when Medea appeals to older gods who were not regularly invoked in Athens, like Helios, Hecate and Ge, she is demonstrating her 'dangerous foreigner' status, as someone with ancient mystical allegiances (Mikalson 1991, pp.83–4).

Key point

Look up the different Greek gods named in the play and think about why they have been invoked. You'll find that most of them have specific associations with oath-keeping, for example, or with women.

We can begin to understand how the Greeks thought about divine influence – especially in well-known myths and hero epics, from which tragedy derived its plots – if we think of 'gods' in terms of what Carl Jung called **archetypes**, rather than seeing them as a boisterous supernatural family of heavyweights on Mount Olympus. An archetype, in Jung's terms, is a primal pattern or model, a collection of impulses we experience psychologically that affects our behaviour and thinking. So, for example, Aphrodite, to whom Medea and the Chorus women refer, can be interpreted as an archetype of what it is to be overcome by 'love' – with all the conflicting positive and negative impulses, emotions and behaviours that 'being in love' can inflict on a helpless mortal. Invoking a god meant calling down powerful life-changing attributes of that dominant archetype, hoping it would take effect in someone's life. Zeus, or Ge, would help you keep an oath, for example. Artemis, the virgin goddess, would protect you and so would Athena, the warlike, justice-giving patroness of the city state. Dionysos, on the other hand, might drive you crazy but could also inspire creativity.

Festival drama

Because drama was an integral part of regional and civic religious festivals, the dedication of performances to the gods was an essential first stage in the proceedings. Plays were offered especially to Dionysos, whose statue was ceremoniously placed in the theatre to watch the performance.

Dionysos

He was the inspirational deity behind religious drama festivals and a god with many attributes. Most commonly associated with the gift of wine and intoxication, and better known by his Roman name, the degenerate party-loving Bacchus, this much-revered god had a strange and dangerous side. He was the god who took possession of the soul, inducing ecstasy in his worshippers (ec-stasis means literally 'standing outside oneself'). Dionysos caused the self-induced frenzy of women in a cult of worshippers called maenads (meaning 'the mad ones'), which Euripides made the basis of his last great play *The Bacchae*, composed twenty-five years after *Medea*.

If we look at his attributes and associations with wild nature, fertility, dance, disguise and shape-shifting, mask-wearing and mystic initiation, we can see that Dionysos is appropriate for drama because he embodies what we still think of as the 'power' of plays to work on the mind and emotions. There could be no more appropriate place than the theatre of Dionysos to explore *Medea*, a play about madness, sexual passion and violent energies. As the Chorus say at the end, anything can happen here: 'What men expect does not happen; for the unexpected, heaven finds a way' (p.87).

The Great, or City, Dionysia

Of all the religious festivals celebrated in Euripides' time, our focus is on the main one, the Great, or City, Dionysia, that attracted both local spectators from around Attica and also strangers, who could attend because the sea was navigable again after winter. Because foreigners would be present, the Great Dionysia was a showcase for the city of

Athens, with comedy, tragedy and satyr plays being performed in the three days of the dramatic competition. (A satyr play was a short play set in the countryside celebrating Dionysos. As far as we know from fragments and images these appear to have been wild and rude!)

The festival week's program

Day 1: the Proagon – the meeting of all personnel taking part in the dramatic contest. There were probably over a thousand men and boys involved – poets, actors, chorus teachers and chorus members, musicians and stagehands – some parading about in purple and gold robes, in a generally spectacular advertisement for the days to come.
Day 2: the Pompe – a ritual procession to the sacred precinct of Dionysos at the Acropolis, with a chorus from each of the ten tribes performing long hymns to Dionysos, called Dithyrambs.
Days 3–5: the dramatic contest – in Euripides' time this spread over the next three days. He, like other tragedians, would submit three tragedies to be played consecutively and a satyr play to round these off. Then each day would end with a comedy by another playwright. This was how the audience first saw Euripides' *Medea* in 431 BC, with *Philoctetes* (now lost), *Dictys* (a few lines left) and *The Reapers*, a satyr play (only fragments left).
Final Day: the Assembly – where everyone gathered together for drama adjudication and the awarding of prizes to the best playwright/director and actors. The **choregos** of the winning entry had a statue put up to honour him and his tribe, since paying all production expenses for his entire team – playwright, chorus trainer, actors, chorus and flute player – was a civic duty worth rewarding.

Greek theatre in performance

Plays were originally performed in the Agora, the civic heart of Athens, but as the population expanded and a temple precinct to Dionysos was established, they shifted in about 500 BC to an amphitheatre on the southern slope of the Acropolis. This theatre was probably wooden scaffolding seats and a wooden back wall to the stage space when Euripides knew it. Some stone structures were built three decades after Euripides' time, but what is left today is what Rome rebuilt, eight hundred years after Euripides.

Key point

Be warned that older books on Greek drama are quite dogmatic about what a 'classical' theatre space looked like, describing a stone building with a circular space for the Chorus. This picture is inaccurate for Euripides, because it is based on surviving theatres like the beautifully proportioned and acoustically magical space at Epidauros, a Greek amphitheatre built two centuries after Euripides' time. (For a conjectural idea of what the theatre may have looked like, see Leacroft 1984, pp.6–15.)

1. **Theatron** – 'the seeing place', originally just a crowd of spectators standing round the orchestra space. Later came a semicircular outdoor auditorium – a Latin word we still use meaning 'a listening place' – with wooden scaffolding, later replaced by stone seating. There were special carved thrones in the front row for officials and priests of Dionysos. Athenian citizens occupied most of the seating, which was probably divided into wedge-shaped blocks for the different tribes, with two outer sections for foreigners and latecomers.
2. **Skene** – from which we get 'scene', originally a hut or tent as a changing room behind the orchestra space for actors to make entrances and exits. Then came a wooden back wall with a central door, which is what *Medea* seems to be using. Stone walls and side structures came after Euripides' time.

There was probably no raised stage at first, or ever. Above the skene – on its flat roof when it became a solid building – was an area where the gods could appear and speak, called the **theologeion**, 'stage of the gods'. This was where the crane, a lever and fulcrum machine, called the **mechane**, was situated. It could 'fly' the gods in and away at the end of the play, and Euripides used it brilliantly for Medea's last exit.

3. Orchestra – the area belonging to the Chorus. There is hot debate about the shape of this area and its connection with the skene space, where the actors are usually placed. It was probably more rectangular than circular to begin with, a large 'dancing place' for the Chorus. In the centre of the space there would have been an altar to Dionysos (**thymele**), a sacrificial step, and a spot where the flute-player (the **aulos**) stood to accompany the Chorus songs (**odes**).

Another hot issue is whether actors were permitted to enter the orchestra in performance – the received view is that the spaces were kept separate but nobody has evidence. Some people argue that it seems like good theatre to bring the **protagonist**, the main actor, and the Chorus close together sometimes – and closer to the audience – in certain passionate exchanges in *Medea*, for example. This would mean invading the Chorus space.

Key point

Think about the parts of a Greek theatre to help you visualise how *Medea* might have been performed in the original space.

The playwrights

Euripides (born Salamis 480 BC, approx.; died Macedonia aged seventy-five, 406 BC) was one of three great tragedians working in what is often thought of as a golden age for drama, with demanding plays encouraging the evolution of professional performers, interesting stage techniques and a specialised performance space. Playwrights not only created tetrarchies of plays, but also composed Chorus music, wrote lyrics for the Odes, choreographed, trained their chorus and directed the whole piece.

Euripides began his theatre career as Aeschylus (d. 456 BC) was coming to the end of his. Aeschylus had performed his own work as the main actor, introducing and training a second, and occasionally a third, to create dialogue between characters, an innovation on the simpler actor/Chorus exchange. Sophocles (d. 406 BC), the other great tragedian, used three actors and increased the Chorus from twelve to fifteen performers. He and Euripides rivalled each other in competition: Sophocles is said to have won first or second prize twenty-four times compared with Euripides' five prizes out of fifty years' work and over ninety plays; Sophocles' tragedy defeated *Medea* in 431 BC.

The performers

Each tragedy would require three speaking actors, a Chorus of fifteen, and a flautist.

1. Chorus To submit your play for the festival was to 'request a chorus', and to have a play accepted was to 'obtain a chorus'. Chorus members, Athenian citizens, had to learn the words, songs and dances for three distinct characterisations (*Medea* requires 'Corinthian women' for instance) and then perform in the satyr play that ended their day in the competition.

2. Actors All performers were male. As they developed skills, actors became professional and were paid out of public funds. The strongest were in great demand, able to hold lead parts in three tragedies in one day and then act in the satyr play at the end. An actor needed a good memory, a strong voice to speak and sing, and facility with gesture and movement. He also needed to be able to adapt quickly to male or female characterisation when role-sharing.

Medea requires three speaking actors, masked and costumed, plus two boys and two adult mutes. The main actor would have to hold the taxing role of Medea throughout, with the second actor probably playing the Nurse and Jason, while the third could be the Tutor, Creon, Aegeus and the Messenger. Alternatively, the second and third actor might share the Nurse and Tutor, and either could perform the Messenger's speech. From what you know of the play, think about what might work best.

The audience

Although it was a citizen's duty to participate, attendance at the Great Dionysia plays was probably about fifty percent on average, giving us an estimate of twelve to fifteen thousand men, including foreign visitors and foreigners who resided in Athens.

Was anyone excluded? There are two groups about whom there is no information: slaves and women. Slaves were sometimes freed at the Great Dionysia, but does that mean that slaves attended plays? Nobody knows. No women took part in any of the organisation of the festival, although at least one young girl was required in the Pompe procession. While there is no evidence for women attending the theatre it doesn't mean they weren't there.

Athenian women and *Medea*

Married women in Athens at this period were constructed as dependents of their husbands, bound to obedience and a sheltered domestic life. Even the names of respectable women weren't to be spoken in public. In Euripides' time, Athenian citizenship for males was dependent on being able to prove double descent, from an Athenian freeborn mother legitimately married to a citizen father. Foreign-born women immediately lost status as potential wives, because their sons would no longer be eligible for citizenship.

By the conventional double standard, men could take any number of sexual partners outside marriage but women were punished severely for adultery. Much attention was paid to women's sexual urges. Athenian men believed that marriage was the way to control women and this message seems to have been underlined in tragic plays. Medea's lack of sex and 'sex-jealousy' are stressed by Jason, for example. Edith Hall notes that:

> women in Athenian tragedy only become disruptive (that is, break one of the 'unwritten laws', act on an inappropriate erotic urge, or flout male authority) in the physical absence of a legitimate husband. (Cited in Easterling 1997, p.106)

Women in general could not participate in any of the activities or civic duties expected of male citizens, and yet, as Hall notes:

> female choruses in the surviving plays outnumber male by twenty-one to ten. Since women were almost excluded from Athenian public life, their prominence in this most public of Athenian art-forms therefore constitutes a problematic paradox. (Easterling, p.105)

Female characters like Medea figured prominently in tragedies performed at the City Dionysia: these plays at least gave expression, through argument, to questions of women's rights and duties, and relationship issues. All actors were male so it must have been a common situation for an actor to play someone like Antigone or Electra or Medea with convincing strength to move the audience, and perhaps thereby to at least recognise the unspoken assumptions of his gendered everyday reality.

GENRE, STYLE & STRUCTURE

Genre

Remember that *Medea* is first of all a **play**, which means it was written for performance, to be heard and seen, rather than to be read silently like a novel. Secondly it's a **tragedy**. We habitually use this word to describe any event that arouses strong emotions, from the sudden death of a celebrity to the collapse of the Australian batting side or a tennis star's defeat. Greek tragedy has a deeply serious purpose – to illustrate the struggle to live as a human being in a hostile world. It has to do with human choices and actions which lead inevitably, even if by accident, to an unhappy ending. Look at the themes *Medea* explores, all deriving from conflict and all leading to suffering.

Style and language

Medea is presented as a long and intense debate between characters with opposing views, chiefly a protagonist (Medea) and antagonist (Jason).

The interest for us goes beyond the debate, since everyone knows the outcome of the story. We listen to how people are thinking about their situation, expressing moral dilemmas, presenting their points of view. It is hard for us not to sympathise with Medea's position but Euripides wants us to listen to Creon, Jason and Aegeus, too, and to hear what ordinary people, such as the Nurse, Tutor and Messenger, have to say.

There is also a debate going on within Medea herself, called a **psychomachia**, a 'battle in the soul'. This is an intense inner conflict between good and evil choices that tears a person apart psychologically. Medea's psychomachia is in Section 15.

John Davie's translation modernises the language to some extent, while still retaining a formality appropriate to the context, genre and style of the original. This enables contemporary audiences to connect with the characters and events without losing the sense of the original work. This translation is in prose (ordinary text with no regular rhythmic pattern), although many translations present the text in verse (with regular rhythm and often rhyme). In the note prefacing the 2003 Penguin edition of the play, Davie states that by writing in prose rather than verse he 'tried to achieve a tone that is more relaxed' (p.xlvi). Think about the other possible effects of the form (verse or prose) in which the text is presented. How does it contribute to our understanding of themes and characters? What is the dramatic impact?

In dialogue, characters use familiar modern language and prose rhythms for realistic effect. One special effect to notice is **stichomythia**, a pattern of dialogue where characters exchange single lines in a rapid sequence, to increase tension in an argument.

More formal patterns of speech indicate a solo lament or a Choric ode which would have been accompanied by the flute.

Structure

Michael Lloyd explains the structure of Greek tragedies in this way:

> Greek tragedies are representations of human action, but also formal structures with internal rules of their own. The possibilities of tension between these two aspects of tragedy are especially evident in the plays of Euripides, which combine realism with a marked formalism of structure. (Lloyd 1992, p.1)

There are no act or scene divisions in *Medea*, but the play moves forward according to a recognisably episodic structure, with interplay between characters and Chorus, and Choric comment in a number of Odes. I have numbered the sections 1–20 in the analysis that follows. (Line numbers refer to the 2003 Penguin Classics edition of the play, in *Medea and Other Plays*, listed in the reference section of this guide.)

SECTION-BY-SECTION ANALYSIS

1. *Prologos* (pp.51–2)

Summary: *The Nurse reminds the audience of the story of Jason and Medea up to their arrival in Corinth. She describes Medea's dangerous state of mind now that Jason has deserted her to marry Creon's daughter.*

Theme cue: betrayal, exile, parents and children, revenge.
The Nurse's first words establish her chatty style but sound as though she is taking up a point in mid-conversation: 'Oh, if only it had never gone ...' (p.51). She is not talking about Medea and the *Argo* at all, in fact, but directing us to catch up with her by asking ourselves 'Who does she mean?' Then we are prompted to recall how Jason and the Argonauts set out long before to raid Colchis, Medea's home, and steal the golden fleece, a sacred object for her people. The Nurse pushes our imagination even further back to reconstruct what she thinks of as the fundamental wrongness of that journey, considering the terrible consequences: she wishes that the very tree which made the boat *Argo* had never been chopped down in the first place. What followed was death for others and exile for Medea 'transfixed by desire for Jason' (p.51).

It is dramatically essential for the Nurse to underline this foreign woman's willing obedience to Jason as his wife – in fact if not in name – because she is about to reveal a terrible change in affairs. Jason has recently married, rejecting outright the very intense devotion that made such a strong personality as Medea's seek 'to please her husband in all she does' in the first place (p.51).

The Nurse registers the devastating effect Jason's betrayal has had on Medea's psyche already, as she lies in 'anguish' within the house, crying and not eating (p.51). Although the audience cannot yet see her, the Nurse describes Medea's state so vividly that we are immediately able to imagine her passionate suffering. All the terrors of being a woman alone, exiled from her homeland, betrayer of her own royal family and, worst of all, alienated from her sons because they are also Jason's children, strike the Nurse forcibly as a prelude to disaster: 'My fear is she may hatch some unheard-of scheme. She is no ordinary woman' (p.52). The Nurse is not blind to her mistress's past faults but pities Medea deeply, and encourages the audience to feel the same.

The Nurse concludes by alerting the audience to the fierce debate they will see unfolding. She expresses a homely kind of compassion for the two children she sees coming onstage: they are innocently oblivious to their mother's suffering, she says, because 'grief knows no place in a child's mind' (p.52). Unlike the Nurse, we know the end of this story already: our sadness is being wound up early in the play as we register the futility of her fearful hopes for young children marked for death.

2. Nurse and Tutor (pp.52–4)

Summary: *The Tutor brings news that Medea is to be exiled. The two old slaves consider who is to blame for the situation.*

Theme cue: betrayal, exile, parent and child, reason and passion, revenge.

As soon as the boys' Tutor joins her onstage, the Nurse reverts to a more homely conversational style of speech. There's a gentle underlying humour in the sight of two old slaves hanging around the front door for a friendly gossip, the Tutor claiming that she's talking ('muttering') to herself about her troubles as usual (p.52). Nonetheless, he listens when the Nurse unburdens herself in a way that we can immediately understand – she just had to get out of the house. Now we know why that prologue began so abruptly. It was expressing her agitation: 'I just had to come out here and tell earth and sky' (p.52).

The Nurse here expresses what the critic Stanford (1983) calls 'compassionate grief' for her mistress. Even though she is a slave, her own heart 'shares the pain' of what Medea is suffering (p.52). The Tutor reluctantly adds another twist to the knife by reporting the gossip that

Creon will banish Medea and her sons. Both slaves are distressed but can do nothing. The Nurse, her loyalties divided, tries to curse Jason, her master, but immediately scolds herself: 'I mustn't say that of my master' (p.53).

Much more pragmatic and hard-headed, the Tutor would like to tell Medea to cease her 'laments' (p.52) and prepare for banishment; in reality they can do nothing to influence events. Besides, Jason's guilt is nothing special in the Tutor's view: 'no one loves his neighbour more than himself' (p.53). Further, notes the Tutor, Jason now 'loves elsewhere' (p.53) so he has ceased to care for his sons.

The Nurse urges the Tutor to keep the children out of their mother's way, as the only safety the two old slaves can provide. Her words 'I've seen her glaring at them like a bull', her anger a 'thunderbolt' (p.53), are chilling.

Key point

This is a shocking moment for the audience, because the two small boys are clearly in view onstage, walking towards the house door in the back wall of the skene. At this very moment we hear Medea's blood-curdling cries of misery from inside, causing the Nurse to repeat her warning: 'don't let her catch sight of you ... Watch out for that savage temperament of hers' (p.53). Will we see them alive again? (Yes, we will, but briefly – and then they will walk through the doors a second time to await their deaths; see p.78.)

The children disappear through the doors and our fears are intensified, especially as we hear the distracted Medea greeting them by calling down death on them. We feel the venom and misery in her words. Any love, for husband, for children, for life itself, has become distorted and negative.

The powerful rhythmic effect of Medea's repetition – 'my sufferings, my wretched sufferings' (p.54) – intensifies the anguish felt by the Nurse and the audience. Once again the Nurse expresses that compassionate grief, mixed with fear, that Aristotle said are the characteristic emotions aroused by tragedy. In order to prevent herself from being overwhelmed, the Nurse reiterates her own belief that 'equal terms' and 'secure and modest circumstances' (p.54) in life are best, because safe and uncomplicated.

3. *Parados* (pp.54–5)

Summary: *The Chorus of Corinthian women enter. They urge the Nurse to fetch Medea out of the house to talk with them.*

Theme cue: betrayal, exile, gender antagonism, appeal to gods for justice.

The Chorus of Corinthian women now take up their position in the orchestra (p.54). There is a sense of urgency in their words, suggesting a quick entrance. They immediately engage the Nurse's attention to tell them about 'the unhappy Colchian' – Medea (p.54).

Medea's eerie lamentation offstage, still out of sight, punctuates the Choric ode, drawing even more intensity from the Corinthian women: 'Did you hear, Zeus and Earth and light, how sad a lament she sings, the sorrowful wife?' (p.54).

The women sympathise but, like the Tutor, they advise acceptance of Jason's behaviour, taking a conventional line that 'If your husband worships a new bride, do not let this fault in him vex you. Zeus will aid you in seeing justice done' (pp.54–5)

Although she agrees with them that 'Zeus, the appointed steward of mortal oaths' (p.55) might listen, the Nurse is less assured that Medea will have the patience to wait for the gods to avenge her.

The Nurse leaves the stage with an extraordinarily reflective but also confronting speech about music. This must stop the audience in its tracks, partly because its meaning is not easy to figure out. It steps beyond the immediate concerns of the play, making us all think about the way music is experienced in life and how it is habitually associated with happy occasions, 'at feasts and banquets and at dinner' (p.55). Her speech draws attention to another potential purpose for music as a healer – but one which, she implies, can never reach the depth of Medea's sorrow.

Those who have written music for celebration did so without 'ever inventing music of song or tuneful lyre to banish the hateful sorrows we mortals know' (p.55).

Key point

This is what is called a meta-theatrical statement, drawing attention to something that is going on in the drama. In this case it makes the audience listen more intently to the actual musical, chanted sounds she and the Chorus and Medea are making in performance – an illustration of music being made not merely to enhance celebrations but to play out a tragedy.

The Nurse then leaves the stage and enters the house, while the Chorus, left alone, conclude their ode by recapitulating the story of Medea's fateful sea journey, and describing her pleas to the gods 'to witness how unjustly she is treated' (p.56).

4. Medea's *Monody* (pp.53–5)

Summary: *Inside the house, Medea expresses her despair and her desire for revenge.*

Theme cue: betrayal (oath-breaking), revenge, family issues.

This mixture of lament and curse punctuates the Chorus/Nurse dialogue onstage three times. Medea's first words are simply sounds of despair: 'Oh, I am wretched … Oh, if only I could die!' (p.53). The same pattern follows when she cries out for a 'flaming bolt from heaven' (p.54) to strike her dead.

Later, Medea urges herself on by reminding herself that her 'noble father [is] the Sun' (p.61), and at the end of the play she will escape in the dragon-drawn chariot that 'the Sun, my father's father' has given her (p.84; in Greek mythology, Medea was the granddaughter of Helios, the sun god). But here, at first, she appeals to the heavens for a quick death, and the audience must see this as a mark of her absolute despair.

Finally, we hear a more formally structured but still passionate speech from Medea, immediately after the Chorus have urged her to accept Jason's behaviour. In fact, by suggesting that she accept, they turn her away from self-destructive thoughts to ideas of active 'revenge'. How fatally they have misread her passionate nature and underestimated both her pain and her powers.

Medea invokes potent energies when she calls upon 'great Themis and lady Artemis' (p.55) to deal with Jason the oath-breaker. The two goddesses are especially significant to her, since Themis, daughter of Ge, Mother Earth, whom Medea venerates, is the personification of the order of things established by law, custom and equity, while Artemis, twin-sister of Apollo, is characterised as both a bringer of sudden deaths, especially to women, *and* a powerful averter of evils.

If Jason has dared to behave in a way that sets him against these cosmic forces, he insults them as well as Medea, who called on them to seal the oaths he made to her. This is the tragic equation Medea draws up and Jason's crime is consequently unpardonable. It not only mocks the gods she holds sacred but, worse than that, makes nonsense of the crimes she committed against her own family and city for Jason's sake. In case the audience has forgotten to keep that connection in mind, Medea herself reiterates her tormenting sense of guilt and loss: 'O Father, O land of Colchis … my own brother's life' (p.55).

She, too, is guilty of having deserted and injured people for the sake of love. The audience begins to perceive a degree of similarity between what Jason has done to Medea and his family, for love, and what Medea did to her family and country for love of him. This complicates our response to her as she articulates the terrible curse on her 'husband … and his bride' (p.55), even though she retains audience sympathy.

5. Entry of the protagonist, Medea (pp.56–7)

Summary: *Medea makes a long speech about being a woman and a foreigner, addressing the Chorus who sympathise with her* *reasonable tone. The Chorus agree to remain silent about any justifiable course of revenge that Medea might find.*

Theme cue: reason in conflict with passion, betrayal, justice (of punishment for Jason).

One way for a playwright to whet an audience's appetite is to hold back and make them wait. Euripides delays his main character's entrance onstage, letting other speakers offer tantalising suggestions about her state of mind. We anticipate what kind of sight she will present, judging from the nature of her cries offstage. We have also been prepared to hear the force of Medea's psychological torment articulated loudly and expect her ferocity and violence to be carried outside, embodied in her presence.

Yet when she steps through the skene doors the stage direction indicates that she enters *'slowly'* and speaks *'in measured tones'* (p.56). Our expectations are not fulfilled so we are even more intrigued. This would have been a genuine shock to the Athenian audience – and a pleasurable surprise. Like the Chorus women, Athenian spectators would not have hesitated in approving of Medea's reasoned exposition of her situation, even though she is both a foreigner *and* a woman expressing criticisms about the uncertain life of women in marriage.

There is passion in this speech, of course, running deep, if we listen to the details – and violence in its intent. Medea is exercising self-control, the much-valued Athenian quality of **sophrosyne**, to manipulate the Chorus into supporting her real aim – to destroy Jason. Medea wins Chorus support by appealing to their generally shared experience of being women. She then moves on to underline her genuine disadvantages, especially in being isolated from the comforts they can still enjoy:

> However, we are not in the same position, you and I. You have your city here and the homes where your fathers have lived; you enjoy life's pleasures and the companionship of those you love. But what of me? Abandoned, homeless, I am a cruel husband's

> plaything ... no mother to turn to, no brother or kinsman to rescue me from this sea of troubles and give me shelter. And so there is one small kindness I ask of you ... (p.57)

The speech turns powerfully on this moment and this half of a sentence. After all, it's only one little request, considering ... of course the Chorus will support her: they agree 'it is just' for Medea to 'take revenge upon' Jason (p.57).

6. *Episodeion I* Creon and Medea (pp.57–60)

Summary: *Because Creon fears what Medea might do to his family, he explains that he must exile her. Medea pleads, and is granted one day to prepare to leave. Exit Creon.*

Theme cue: reason and passion control people's lives; parents and children.

Creon's dialogue with Medea is the first main dramatic 'episode' and introduces the second main actor (the **deuteragonist**) on the skene. Through the Tutor's gossip, we have an idea what news Creon will be bringing. His blunt insistence that he must exile Medea and her sons stems from fear that she is 'no stranger to dark knowledge' (p.58). Medea is deeply insulted by his attack on her 'reputation' (p.58) which, she knows, stems from how she has used her intelligence; this has led to her 'serious harm' and made her a 'victim' (p.58).

If you look back at Medea's entrance speech, you will see that she herself has already explained to the Chorus why she needs to rely on her magic arts to survive:

> Once she finds herself among customs and laws that are unfamiliar, a woman must turn prophet to know what sort of man she will be dealing with as husband – not information gained at home. (p.56)

This is special pleading, perhaps, designed to get the Chorus on side about an issue they know to be a problem for all women, but there's more than a grain of truth in it as well. Medea's arts, extending beyond sex magic, have helped Jason to achieve his heroic successes in the past. Her cleverness has certainly been to his advantage. And now Creon pinpoints that very quality in Medea to justify exiling her again.

It is a sign of Medea's fierce intelligence working at this moment that, despite being enraged and insulted, she pretends to see Creon's point. She deflects the force of his accusation by pretending to accept culpability for using her brains: 'Any man of good sense should never have his children taught to be unusually clever' (p.58) she claims, before pointing out a string of disadvantages, including the jealousy and dislike of less intelligent people.

While what she argues sounds plausible, and the audience would probably be nodding their heads in agreement, we also register the suppressed mockery in her tone. She clinches her argument by appealing directly to Creon's status in relation to hers: 'Have no fear of me, Creon; my circumstances at present do not encourage me to offend against kings!' (p.58). Again, the Athenian audience might consider this true. But her strategy backfires this time, as Creon instinctively suspects her calmness: 'A woman who is hot-tempered, and likewise a man, is easier to guard against than one who is clever and controls her tongue' (pp.58–9).

Key point

It is essential that Medea gains time to put her revenge into operation. She must find a way to break Creon's resolve, and so she tries again, this time hitting what really motivates him – family feelings.

Now follows a fast-paced dialogue consisting of single lines, a pattern called **stichomythia**. For Medea, it is not just a matter of skilful argument to get what she wants. We must feel her desperation, too. This is her last chance to gain time so she touches on points that give her anguish to put into words: her lost country and love betrayed. She pulls out all the stops to prevent Creon from calling his guards – and at last she hits on Creon's fatal emotional weakness, his fatherly love. He gives her a day's grace to plan a new 'start in life' for her sons (p.59), little guessing how costly it will prove to him and his family. The audience begins to feel the tension of complicated feelings. Medea is not arguing in her children's best interests but using them as emotional levers to manipulate Creon. Euripides makes us wait a while longer to discover her true feelings for them.

7. Medea and Chorus (pp.60–2)

Summary: *Medea expresses her contempt for Creon, repeats her desire for revenge and invokes the goddess Hecate. The Choric ode supports her, because the world has turned from honourable values.*

Theme cues: reason and passion, betrayal (love dishonoured), gender antagonism.

As Creon leaves, the Chorus-Leader takes up a pitying lamentation for Medea's imminent exile: 'Oh, a god has launched you on a sea of troubles' (p.60).

Medea's tone in her next long speech (another monody, although she is sometimes addressing the Chorus) is anything but lamenting. In fact, the audience might experience an uncomfortable shock to find her so cool-headed after the previous passionate exchange with Creon. Have we all been duped again? She turns mockingly on the naive group of Corinthian women: 'Do you imagine I would ever have stooped to flattery of this man without having some profit, some scheme in mind?' (p.60).

Then follows a passionate and fearful monologue, in which Medea visualises how she will exact revenge on 'father, daughter and husband – my husband!' (p.60); 'Not one of them will live to boast of vexing my heart' (p.61).

For the first time in the play the Athenian audience experienced here the forceful picture of a 'foreign' mind and heart, guaranteed to terrify them. Medea would like Fate to be on her side but if she must do the murders on her own, including the possibility of killing her two children, then she knows she is resourceful enough to proceed unaided.

Key point

Medea's decision to 'delay for just a short while' in case she might 'find someone to support' her (p.61) sounds like good sense, but it serves another less obvious dramatic purpose for Euripides. The playwright is aware of his Athenian audience's sense of security in their 'civilised' society. Medea's 'support' will soon appear in the form of Aegeus, King of Athens, which will give the audience a great deal to puzzle over. (See further discussion in Section 10 below.)

The audience, then and now, must be further disturbed by Medea's appeal to Hecate (p.61), revealing her dangerously magical nature and powers. Athenians venerated Hecate, an ancient mysterious goddess, by leaving out dishes of food at places where two roads crossed (her dwelling places) at the end of every month. She was the goddess who was there at points of change, of 'crossing over'. Hecate, they knew, taught sorcery and was the dark aspect of Artemis, with powers over the moon, the earth and the underworld. And she is Medea's 'chosen accomplice' (p.61), invoked in a trance-like prayer that becomes more and more intense. Medea works herself into a state of mind capable of achieving superhuman acts, identifying herself proudly as semi-divine: 'you whose noble father is the Sun ... You have the knowledge', and therefore not to be mocked by 'Jason and his Sisyphean wedding' (p.61).

And then, as she is in mid-flight, there is a brilliant dramatic shift in tone. Medea remembers that the female Chorus are present, listening. The word 'we' marks the moment where she directs her attention again to the ordinary human women with a statement heavily laced with irony in justification of her plans: 'we are women, quite helpless in doing good but surpassing any master craftsman in working evil' (p.61).

The Chorus ode refutes what Medea has just claimed (demonstrating that they fully understood her irony), asserting that the world has turned upside down, not just through women, but because of men's deceitful and faithless ways. Men prove to be as bad as women – but because women don't write ballads or poems nobody remembers the stories. Euripides is helping to redress the balance through this play, perhaps:

a man writing in defence of women? (See 'Athenian women and *Medea*' in the Background & Context section.)

Key point

The ode orientates us in preparation for the key scene coming up – the agon. At last Jason, already painted as the villain and Medea's opponent, the antagonist, will be able to speak in his own defence.

8. *The Agon* Jason and Medea (pp.62–7)

Summary: *Jason enters. He blames Medea for causing her own banishment through her temper, jealousy and refusal to accept the situation. Medea accuses him of betrayal and ingratitude. Jason is pragmatic, reminding Medea that they are now living in a civilised country not in her barbarous old world. Exit Jason.*

Theme cue: All the main issues surface in the agon arguments. Both Jason and Medea argue from what they consider to be strong positions.

Key point

The agon is what the audience has been waiting for, because it brings together the two great opponents in a formally recognised debate pattern. Each character makes a long defensive speech, with two or three Choric interjections, and then characters argue more intensely (stichomythia) before spinning apart furiously at the end of the agon. And, of course, the point of the tragedy is that it is too late for the agon to have any effect because Jason has already deserted Medea and married Glauce.

Jason's first speech is a prologue to the agon proper, designed by him to shift blame by reproving Medea for what she has brought on herself but, dramatically, having the effect of reminding the audience of something else that evokes pity for her – the reality of banishment. In one speech (p.62) he repeatedly draws attention to this fate – 'exile', 'reward', 'banishment', 'punishment', 'arguing for your continued stay', 'cannot be a home' – before offering help 'to prevent your being driven out together with our children ... penniless' (p.62). The audience must be struck immediately by the inadequacy of Jason's offer, knowing the strength and complexity of Medea's passion.

Medea's long speech is a combination of cool rhetorical sophistication and bitter passion. In her introduction (called formally the **proem**) she insults Jason then comments self-reflexively on what she's doing, on her inability to describe him as harshly as she would like: 'my tongue can utter no worse abuse against your spinelessness' (p.62).

After restating the history that they have shared, Medea appeals to the man who is the father of her children. At the heart of her argument is the twofold accusation that Jason has broken faith with her and, by dishonouring his oath, has dishonoured the gods:

> For if you still had no sons, it would be something I could forgive, this desire you have for a new bride. Gone is the trust to be placed in oaths; I cannot discover if you think that the gods you swore by then have lost their sovereignty or that new laws these days are prescribed for men ... (p.63)

Buried deep in her accusation is Medea's own sense of guilt: 'I betrayed my own father, my own family to come here with you' and 'to please you, I have become hated by the very people who should have had kindness from me, not harm' (p.63). Conjuring up the fearful image of herself and the children wandering 'as beggars' (p.64), Medea appeals to the gods to account for the mistake she made in choosing Jason:

> O Zeus, why is it you have given men clear ways of testing whether gold is counterfeit but, when it comes to men, the body carries no stamp of nature for distinguishing bad from good? (p.64)

No godlike answer is forthcoming, of course: she ends her speech and the Chorus underline how Medea's rage stems proportionately from the strength of love.

Will Jason's feelings be represented as strongly? His speech begins with a jauntily inappropriate image of seamanship about riding out the hurricane. We silently compare this with the way the Chorus and Medea use the same imagery, always associated seriously with danger, exile and loss.

Jason undercuts everything that Medea values in her life so that we see the tragic conflict between her passionate rage and his cold pragmatism, which must necessarily devalue her part in his life. He infuriates Medea because he stresses the virtues of governed emotions, sensible provision for life – putting status and marital security before private feelings – and civilised law to control human conduct. These are all things Medea has foregone, rejected or overthrown in her love for Jason. In fact, she tells him how much she despises his sensible provisions: 'I only hope I may never enjoy a life of prosperity that brings pain or a happiness that would torment my heart' (p.66).

Jason calmly informs Medea 'you gained more than you gave' (p.64), pointing out the advantages she has enjoyed through alliance with him – civilisation in place of barbarity, justice, law instead of force, even fame! Whether he is aware of it or not, and we assume he is insensitive to the effects of his reasoned argument on her, Jason insults Medea with every word. He finally impugns her very womanhood: 'what need have you of children?', complaining that 'There should have been some other means for mankind to reproduce itself, without the need of a female sex; this would rid the world of all its troubles' (p.65).

One of the most painful moments in this play is when Jason tries to gloss over his contribution to Medea's outrage by sneeringly calling it 'jealousy', with the implication that Medea – indeed, like all women – is jealous of his masculinity (p.65). We are in the position to understand Medea's state of mind and feel intense sympathy when she attacks his 'tongue's ability to dress his foul thoughts in fair words' (p.65). The Chorus-Leader also agrees that Jason has acted wrongly, even though it may 'surprise' him not to have won the support of the Chorus (p.65). Corinth was a city that, like Athens, thought of itself as civilised.

Nonetheless, the Corinthian women here are not swayed by Jason's 'rational' argument. Athenian citizens – possibly all men – in the audience, too, would have had to consider Jason a difficult test case.

The agon ends in mutual recriminations. Jason and Medea look at the world and judge life according to their own set of ideas about the purpose of relationships, power, honour and security. Their views are utterly irreconcilable. Jason tries to the bitter end to offer his kind of support, given that he accepts the reality of the situation: 'If you refuse this offer you are mad, my lady' (p.66). In the end he gives up, invoking 'the gods to witness' that he is 'willing to do anything' for both Medea and their sons (p.67). Medea's words follow a similar pattern but she refuses to even accept his self-serving notion of reality and ends by invoking the gods to curse Jason's marriage as one he 'will have cause to lament' (p.67).

9. Choric Ode (p.67)

Summary: *The Chorus reflect on Aphrodite's wonderful but dangerous power. They remind us of Medea's plight by imagining themselves in her position. Finally they acknowledge sadly that their own city, Corinth, has also failed to pity the exile.*

Theme cue: people's vulnerability to the power of love, of being overcome by passion; exile and betrayal.

Athenians believed that Aphrodite, the goddess of love and beauty, could exercise awesome but unpredictable powers in a person's life: they knew how influential she had been among heroes in the well-known stories of Greek epic literature. Named after her home on the island of Cyprus, the 'dread Cyprian' (p.67) could spread chaos among civilised communities. So when the Choric ode, reflecting on what has just happened to Medea and Jason, picks up the theme of dangerous love, the audience is encouraged to share possibilities that can arouse real fears.

The Chorus plead for a quiet life, to be untouched by Aphrodite's 'unerring' golden arrow of love, fired from the bow of her son Eros (p.67).

But if it is 'unerring', then the unspoken question of who can be safe from it hangs in the air. Anyone can become crazy through love. Who would want to have a peaceful domestic life ruined, or to become an 'exile, living that helpless, wearisome life ... denied one's native land' (p.67) if they could help it? The Chorus women lament over Medea, an example of these twin disasters standing before them.

Whatever persuasive force Jason's argument may have had among the audience earlier, the Choric ode forcefully reaffirms his shame: 'Untouched by grace or favour may he die, the man who cannot honour his loved ones ... Never shall he be friend of mine' (p.67).

10. *Episodeion II* Aegeus and Medea (pp.67–71)

Summary: *Aegeus, returning from the Oracle of Apollo at Delphi where he has been asking to be made fertile, offers friendship to Medea. She offers to help him if, in return, he will give her sanctuary in Athens. He agrees that Athens will shelter her if she can escape Corinth by her own efforts. She makes him swear to the agreement by the old gods she honours. Exit Aegeus.*

Theme cue: gender harmony, exile, parents and children – family issues. The Choric ode ends on a note of great sadness but the dramatic mood is changed instantly by the entrance of Aegeus with his positive greeting, 'Medea, I wish you joy' (p.68). This is not intended ironically: they really do greet each other enthusiastically as 'friends' (p.68), and Aegeus compliments Medea on her intelligence by actively seeking her advice on the puzzling answer he has been given by the oracle, saying 'a shrewd mind is what is needed' (p.68).

Aegeus is presented to us as a kind man. When he notices that Medea is looking 'pale and wasted' he asks her what is wrong (p.68). When she tells him about Jason and her exile, he continues to listen and be supportive. Medea proposes to use her medical skills to make Aegeus fertile and, in return, begs for sanctuary. To her relief, he agrees.

Key point

This is a peripeteia, or reversal of fortune, a real turning point for the whole play. Aegeus, representing Athens, is the answer to Medea's wish for 'someone to support' her (p.61) and will enable her to pursue her revenge and survive.

His tactics show Aegeus to be a shrewd diplomat, a man who uses his reason carefully. He does not wish to give offence to his Corinthian friends by aiding Medea openly while she is still in Corinth, but if she can find her way to Athens by her own efforts, she is guaranteed safety. When she agrees, and proposes sealing the agreement with a sacred oath, Aegeus is quite ready to bind himself because it will be useful to him politically. He is 'quite prepared to carry it out' because it 'involves [him] in less risk' and he will have an 'excuse' to offer those who might criticise his action (p.70).

Aegeus may not understand the fundamentally sacred nature of oath-taking as Medea does, but we are sure that he, unlike Jason, will respect a promise to the gods. He binds himself specifically, according to Medea's instructions, by Earth, by the ancient goddess Ge, and by the sun, Helios, the god who sees and hears everything. If he breaks his word, he vows to suffer the 'fate awaiting mortals who offend against the gods' (p.71). Again we are reminded of Jason the oath-breaker, the guilty man. Will the gods find a way to punish him? Is Aegeus himself, by helping Medea, an instrument in the hands of the unseen and unknowable gods? These questions start to surface in the minds of the audience.

Euripides introduces Aegeus into the play for three main reasons. Firstly, his offer of shelter in Athens promises Medea the security she will need after carrying out the terrible revenge she proposes, and so clears the way for her to proceed.

Secondly, Aegeus represents another aspect of family dynastic concerns, another central theme; he is a ruler without heirs. Just as Medea decides that she will have to destroy Jason's children to complete her revenge, she also promises to ensure fertility to Aegeus, to help establish his family line. Aegeus has been to Apollo's oracle at Delphi to ask how he might 'father offspring' (p.68). It is through Medea that his wish will be granted. She will be Apollo's agent as far as Aegeus is concerned and she will be the bearer of one of his future sons, too.

Thirdly, Aegeus represents Athens, the Attic state, the epitome of rational life and civilisation in the minds of the original audience. Knowing that he's offering Medea support is likely to complicate the audience's response to her and her actions even more. The greatest challenge to the Athenian citizens among the original audience at the Great Dionysia would have been to acknowledge that a historical king of Athens could be confessing to sterility onstage, raising uncomfortable doubts about the fabled perfection of life in the city state.

This episode would have been full of local interest to the original audience. For us, it shows that one honourable man, the representative of Athens itself, can treat Medea decently and respect her cleverness, contrasting both with Creon's fear of her power that leads to cruelty, and Jason's reductive and misogynistic opinion of her.

11. Medea and Chorus (pp.71–3)

Summary: *Medea reveals her plan for revenge on Jason's new bride, Glauce (Creon's daughter), and then on Jason himself, by killing his two sons. The Nurse overhears Medea's terrible determination. Medea sends the Nurse to fetch Jason. The Choric ode comments on the greatness of Athens and on Medea's planned course of action.*

Theme cue: exile and belonging, the harmony of civilised life, offending the gods, pollution of the sacred, parents and children.

Alone again with the Chorus, who have expressed their approval of Aegeus' 'noble heart' (p.71), Medea exults in her good fortune in an outburst of excitement. She calls out a half-formed prayer of praise to the gods: 'Zeus! Justice, child of Zeus! Light of the Sun!' (p.71). This is in striking contrast to her earlier woeful cries to the gods from inside the house.

Her excitement continues, because Medea knows this is her chance to take revenge – but she must act quickly. Her words underline for the audience that Aegeus has turned her fortune around: 'This man has shown himself a haven to my plans, just when my ship was rolling in heavy seas. To him I shall fasten my stern cable' (p.71).

For the first time, Medea uses that recurrent imagery of the sea in a positive way, suggesting security rather than exile.

Medea now proceeds with her long solo, directly addressing the Chorus: 'Now I will tell you all my plans' (p.71). As she visualises the steps of her strategy to destroy Glauce, Medea withdraws into a passionately intense kind of self-absorption, bordering on madness in its attention to detail. 'But now I dismiss this business from my thoughts' (p.71) suggests that Medea suddenly becomes aware of how sadistically self-indulgent she is allowing herself to be. And the next painful step of the revenge that comes into her thoughts forces her excitement to subside completely: 'I shall kill my own children' (p.71). Medea is never for a moment in doubt as to the horror of this act, the 'havoc' she will wreak (p.71). Her justification, she claims, is the depth of her love, mixed with pride: she won't allow anyone to take her 'beloved children' from her and the 'mockery' of her enemies is something she 'will not tolerate' (pp.71–2).

Medea's tone at the end of her speech is quite different from how she began. Familiar feelings of exile and despair drag down her mood and harden her deadly resolve because she knows she has nothing more to lose. The audience, originally made up largely of Greeks who set great store on language and debate, are here informed that she was destroyed when first she followed Jason, 'persuaded by the words of a Greek' (p.72). Now, she herself will use 'honeyed words' (p.71) to deceive Jason and enact her plans.

The Chorus-Leader pinpoints the audience's dilemma here, wanting to support Medea but also anxious to uphold 'mankind's laws' (p.72). They focus our attention unwaveringly on the emotional cost of Medea's plan even to herself: 'no woman would then know greater misery' (p.72).

Medea cuts off further debate, sending the Nurse, who has been waiting in sight of the audience throughout Medea's speech, to fetch Jason. He will unknowingly set her plan in motion. As she leaves, the Chorus begin their ode in praise of Athens, the city of prosperous harmony, where love – 'the Cyprian' – and the rational life – 'Wisdom' – coexist.

The first two stanzas of the ode strike such a contrasting picture of a 'civilised' way of life, compared to Medea's experience of violent and passionate upheavals. The Chorus is presenting to the Athenian audience their ideal picture of their own democratic city. This is how Athens wanted to see itself represented to the world, especially at a big public festival where foreigners would be present to take in the message. It has been argued that Euripides may well have been suggesting that Athenians listen and then take a good hard look at the everyday reality of their world, far from ideal, and perhaps not so unlike Medea's. The purpose seems to be to forestall the audience's outright condemnation of Medea, which would be too simple a response.

In the final two stanzas of the ode, the Chorus turn their attention directly to Medea. How will she fit into the harmony of Athens when she takes sanctuary there? Where will she find the 'boldness' for the task (p.73)? And how will she bear the pain of killing her own children? Significantly, Medea remains silent. Her firm resolve to proceed and the depths of her inner feelings are demonstrated in the episode that follows with Jason.

12. *Episodeion III* Jason and Medea (pp.73–6)

Summary: *Jason returns. Medea appears to agree with Jason's 'good judgement' – he's right after all. Jason accepts her change of heart as sensible, saying he will provide for the children in the future. He agrees to let the children take Medea's gift of clothing to Glauce. Exit Jason, with Tutor and the boys.*

Theme cue: reason against passion, betrayal – deception, revenge.
Like the Chorus, we listen to Medea's placatory speech and, briefly, hear her rational summary of the situation from Jason's point of view.

But we recognise that her words are a bitter parody of what he considers to be good sense. This is the central test of Medea's tragic resolve, and all her emotional strength and intelligence are required to accomplish her plan: she must convince Jason that she means every word she utters. We experience, with fascinated horror, her cunning manipulation of Jason. We also register the stress that she is experiencing. Twice in the episode she breaks down weeping. Jason, failing to comprehend the trigger each time – the children and their future – brusquely dismisses her distress: 'It is too much!' (p.75). Medea's thoughts are on her children, now beside her onstage with Jason. She feels compelled to kill them in order to wound Jason most deeply, but the strain of this moment almost overwhelms her. On the one hand, she is perfectly in control of herself, able to calculate the effect of every word, as in: 'Come out and give us your greeting! Join me in saying goodbye to your father and share with your mother her change of heart ... bitterness has gone' (p.74). On the other hand, she cannot maintain her calm demeanour when Jason makes his sweepingly confident claim about the children's secure future with him in Corinth:

> As for you, children, your father has shown himself no fool in working to achieve – the gods willing – your perfect safety ... your father and whatever friends he has in heaven will see to the rest. (p.74)

At this Medea breaks down, weeping, because she knows otherwise. She goes on to practise deceit on the children she loves because they must be the instruments of her revenge. She needs to persuade Jason to let the boys take her golden robes, family treasures from the Sun-god Helios (p.75), to the new bride. Medea's robes are divinely charged because they belong to her, a sun-gift which will burn Glauce, the usurper of Medea's position.

Jason's insultingly arrogant dismissal of her gifts doesn't faze Medea; she merely redoubles her flattery. Medea's deadly calculation is pitted against Jason's lack of feeling and his smug assumption that she has finally, but quite naturally, capitulated to his greater sense. It is Jason's fatal error to take Medea's illusion of obedience to him for the reality. As he deceived her in a fundamental way, so now she turns the tables by the same degree of deception.

13. Choric Ode (p.76)

Summary: *A lament; there's no more hope for the children, or for Glauce, Jason and Medea.*

Theme cue: Justice or revenge, parents and children, reason against passion.

As Jason and the children, with their Tutor, leave the skene, the Chorus break into an anguished lament for the inevitable tragedy about to happen. Their words link everyone in the tragic web. The innocent children are 'going to embrace a bloody death' (p.76), carrying Medea's poisoned robes to the doomed bride. The chorus pity Jason – 'bridegroom of sorrow' (p.76) – but recognise his fatal confidence in his own good sense: 'Wretched man … indeed deceived in your destiny' (p.76). Finally they weep for Medea, the 'pitiful mother of sons', and for what she is committed to do to 'avenge' her 'bridal bed' (p.76).

This ode is sad but reflective, the calm before the storm. It invites the audience to recognise that in a tragedy everyone suffers, even the innocent, through human faults of ignorance or wilfulness. We are being prepared to bear the emotional weight of what is imminent.

14. Tutor and Medea (pp.76–7)

Summary: *The Tutor returns from the palace with news that Glauce was delighted with Medea's gifts and will take Medea's two children into her protection. Medea weeps. The Tutor is puzzled by this response. Isn't she pleased that the children won't be banished?*

Theme cue: revenge and tragic inevitability, passion versus reason.

Euripides creates another wonderful small dramatic moment here, changing the mood in an unexpected way. The audience, knowing the story, is expecting dire news of slaughter from Creon's palace. But the Tutor returns with quite a contrary message: Glauce loves Medea's gifts and will gladly reprieve the children from banishment. Notice the juxtaposition of the Tutor's report that 'your little ones are under no threat' (p.76) with Medea's distress.

Medea understands the full tragic irony of this situation, in that the only enemy to her children now is herself, their mother. Her response is 'Oh, misery!' (p.76), and again, seconds later, 'Oh, misery, I say, misery!' (p.77). This is the beginning of Medea's tragic **psychomachia**, the battle in the soul. She acknowledges to the Tutor that: 'This is what the gods and I devised, I and my foolish heart' (p.77).

Assuming that she is upset at the thought of exile for herself, the Tutor offers rough but kindly-meant comfort: 'your children shall surely have you restored ... You are not alone in being separated from your children' (p.77). He goes indoors, perplexed, to follow Medea's orders to 'prepare their daily food for the children' (p.77).

15. Medea and Chorus (pp.77–8)

Summary: *Medea's psychomachia: she justifies why she will kill the children, weighing her great love for them against her hatred of Jason.*

Theme cue: the maximum tension between passion and reason for Medea.

Another impressive and heart-rending theatrical solo follows from Medea as she battles within herself to decide what to do: to kill or not to kill her two children. At first, she gives the impression that she's weeping because, while she will be alone in exile, her sons will grow up and marry before she can 'take any pleasure' in them or witness their 'happiness' (p.77). Nor will they be able to care for her when she becomes old, or, when she dies, perform the proper funeral rituals for her body. She expresses her shattered hopes: 'that thought and its sweet comfort are no more' (p.77).

Her anguish is palpable to the audience. But embedded in Medea's personality is the paradox of a mother's breaking heart side by side with a hard heart which is full of pride and hatred, something she acknowledges: 'Oh, this stubborn heart of mine! What misery it has cost me!' (p.77).

While the Chorus listen in silence, Medea swings from feeling the horror ('I could not do it ... bringing suffering on them to cause their father pain') to stern rationalisation ('what is the matter with me? Do I want to become a laughing-stock by letting my enemies off scot-free?') and back again ('stop, my heart, do not do this deed!'), finally settling on the argument that she must be cruel to be kind: 'I will not leave my children to the mockery of my enemies' (p.78).

Euripides powerfully manipulates the audience's emotions by juxtaposing the images of cold-blooded murder with Medea's gentle, motherly affection: 'my children, my pretty ones ... O how I love to hug them! The softness of their skin, the sweetness of their breath, my darling ones!' (p.78).

Medea finally acknowledges the supremacy of her anger. The chillingly still point comes with her words to the Chorus, immediately after the children have left, indicating that she accepts responsibility in full awareness: 'I am well aware how terrible a crime I am about to commit, but my passion is master of my reason, passion that causes the greatest suffering in the world' (p.78).

16. Choric Ode (pp.78–9)

Summary: *The Corinthian women reflect on the blessings of childlessness and the misfortune of having children.*

Theme cue: parents, children and domestic life; justice, the gods and suffering; the woman's voice.

Unable to dissuade Medea from her final decision, the Chorus sing a sad but icy lament on parenthood, inverting conventional ideas about children as a blessing. They preface their views with an apologetic reflection on the difficulties of them expressing opinions at all, since they are women.

Why do they have to stress this point, with almost comic exaggeration? In the original performance, remember, the Chorus addressed an audience largely comprising Athenian men, who held the conventionally negative ideas of their time about the capacity, let alone the right, of women to formulate and express views of any kind – especially in public debate. The audience is being told to listen, to take notice. Originally, the Chorus playing Corinthian women were all male performers in costumes and masks. This might have helped the audience to focus on the issue, without being sidetracked by worrying about women getting too bold, and to recognise that the Chorus voices were speaking from a woman's perspective about the difficulties of raising children, an issue that might concern both men and women and be worth thinking about.

The subject matter of this ode is another challenge to an audience, past and present. The Chorus put a case against taking on the burden of creating a family, the very basis of established citizen life, associated with social status and power through heirs. Creon, Jason and Aegeus are all obsessed with founding, preserving and protecting a royal dynasty that is theirs and that gives them meaning. Medea has, literally, destroyed her own royal family and another one that rivalled Jason's family interests. Her central reason for killing the children is to eradicate Jason's dynasty. Don't forget that even as the Choric ode is being performed, another royal family, Creon's, is dying by Medea's poison. Death, as the Chorus point out, may strike down children at any time, so 'what profit is it, then, to mankind, that the gods should cast upon them, to crown their other woes, this bitterest sorrow, all for the love of sons?' (p.79).

Through this ode Euripides returns our focus to the distorted anguish of Medea's state of mind, which has closed itself to maternal impulses. Death is now very close to Medea's own children.

17. Messenger speech (pp.79–82)

Summary: *A Messenger enters with terrible news from the palace, urging Medea to escape quickly. His long descriptive speech vividly recounts how Glauce and Creon died by Medea's fiery poisoned garments. Exit Messenger.*

Theme cue: betrayal – this time Medea's treachery; revenge – its tragic necessity; parents and children.

Rushing onstage, the Messenger shatters the quieter mood of the ode. Medea has been waiting to hear this news; the delay has wound up audience tension, too. His first impulse is to warn Medea to get away but she insists on hearing every detail of the ghastly deaths she has caused. Speaking for ordinary folk, the household slaves who have been with Jason in Creon's palace, he notes: 'we servants who had sympathised with you in your troubles were pleased' to receive the children and to hear how Medea and Jason had 'mended' their 'quarrel of earlier days' (p.80). He omits no detail of Glauce's acceptance of the children when Jason presented Medea's beautiful gifts and how she took pleasure in dressing herself in the golden coronet and robes afterwards.

There is something supernatural about the way the poison took effect as the Messenger describes it. Medea's gifts seem to have been imbued with the power of the Sun-god, as the coronet 'released a wondrous stream of devouring fire' (p.81). Each time Glauce 'shook her head, the flame burned twice as fiercely' (p.81). The Messenger's graphic description works on the audience's imagination and we see it all vividly re-created.

You will sometimes read that it was forbidden to show violent acts onstage in Greek tragedy. While it's true that onstage deaths are rare in surviving plays there seems to have been no hard and fast rule about this, although showing deaths might have been taboo for superstitious reasons. I'm inclined to agree with Pat Easterling (1997, p.154) when she suggests that playwrights like Euripides deliberately used Messenger speeches to enhance the dramatic power of the moment, 'making creative choices for positive reasons'. The Messenger's speech in *Medea* makes our imagination work overtime to evoke the horrible scene in Creon's palace. Then we cope with the horror by thinking about it. Moments later, we *know* that Medea is killing the boys because we hear them crying – but, like the Chorus, we are shut out at the crucial moment, having to imagine what's going on and thinking about why it's happening. Classic horror films work like this: often what you don't see has a stronger effect than what you do see.

The shocked Messenger concludes his speech with a pessimistic view of life: in the end he thinks of it as 'a shadow' and, despite any amount of good fortune, 'no one in this life of ours knows happiness' (p.82).

18. Medea and the Chorus (pp.82–3)

Summary: *Medea resolves to kill her children and enters the house. The Chorus appeal to Earth and the Sun to prevent murder. Hearing the children's cries, the Chorus wonder whether they should act to prevent the killing, but they do nothing.*

Theme cue: parents and children – murder of own blood; passion.
Having completed the first stage of her revenge, Medea is committed to the final action – to destroy Jason by killing his children. In her disturbing speech to the Chorus about the inevitability of her children's deaths, Medea reasons that, since the children will now be targets for revenge, she is protecting them from greater violence. Nonetheless, in her imagination she sees her 'wretched hand' take up a sword, as she moves to the 'starting line' of a 'painful race' (p.82). The deliberate way she speaks, detailing every step, willing herself to do something that is horrifying to her, indicates her profound reluctance. Her last words before entering the house reflect the anguish of tragic resignation. They remind us again that every decision she has made as a consequence of her love for Jason has led finally to this – child murder: 'Oh, I am a woman born to sorrow!' (p.82).

The Chorus women reach a frenzy of grief for the waste of life, the enormity of Medea's crime and the likely consequences, as they listen to the children's cries. Unable to prevent Medea from carrying out her plan, the women marvel at her strength: 'you are made of rock or of iron' (p.83).

There are two other points to notice in this Choric ode. First, the women underline Medea's situation by comparing her with the mythical figure of Ino, also an exile and child-murderer, who was driven insane by misery and guilt to end her own life. They speculate on the divine punishment Medea is calling down on herself by killing children descended from the Sun-god, since she is committing an act of sacrilege by spilling 'the blood of a god' (pp.82–3). Like the Chorus, the audience wonders, 'What further horror could match this?' (p.83).

The second point to notice is how the Chorus have subtly realigned themselves with ideas and beliefs that an original audience would be likely to share. Before, they tended to voice support for Medea; now they withdraw. Child-murder, conventionally, is bound to lead to terrible repercussions and the 'sorrows that heaven wills' upon the 'houses' of those who commit it (p.83), especially when it is a crime against the gods, especially perpetrated by a vengeful woman. The Chorus conclude the ode by underlining the part women play in tragic events: 'Oh, how many the troubles caused by the loves of women! How many sorrows you have brought on mankind before now!' (p.83). The audience waits to find out what kind of punishment will come to Medea.

Key point

This is likely to be a point of contention for modern audiences who are less willing to accept generalisations about 'women'. Furthermore, Medea's history, motivations and relationships are compounding factors in a complex tragedy.

19. *Episodeion IV* Jason with Medea (pp.83–7)

Summary: *Jason enters, distraught, and the Chorus tell him that Medea has killed the boys. As Jason batters at the skene doors, Medea appears above the skene: a 'deus ex machina', in a Sun-chariot drawn by* *dragons. Beside her are the children's bodies. She refuses to give them to Jason but will take them to Athens for burial. After a final vicious argument, Jason is left cursing as the chariot moves out of sight.*

Theme cue: justice conflicts with revenge, gender antagonism, parents and children.

The first significant thing to notice in this last episode is how theatrically spectacular it is when Euripides springs his final surprise on the audience. The Chorus-Leader directs our eyes to the skene door by instructing Jason to 'Open the doors and you will see your murdered children' (p.84). Immediately he calls: 'remove the bars, undo the fastenings! I want to see this double catastrophe!' (p.84). Will the doors open and show us all the horror? Sometimes at this point in a tragedy the skene doors would be opened so that a wooden trolley construction, called the **ekkeklema**, could be wheeled out and on it dead bodies could be displayed. It allowed the 'inside' scene to be brought 'outside' for everyone to see: but not this time.

Jason expects to find himself face to face with a murderous woman but Medea, more powerful than ever, reveals her semi-divine nature to the entire theatre as she rises above the skene in a fantastic chariot provided by her grandfather, the Sun-god. Euripides brilliantly uses the other main device available to Greek theatre, the **mechana**, or crane. Now Medea is removed from the worldly level of Jason, who stands impotently 'grounded' with the Chorus of Corinthian women below. She looks down at him with all the triumph and contempt of a goddess, unconcerned by his curses.

Key point

Medea appears as a 'deus ex machina', the god from the machine, familiar to the Greek audience as a divinity who would be seen to overlook the action and sometimes intervene to bring things to a close at the end of a tragedy, when humans were incapable of resolving issues. It is not possible to know how this last scene actually looked in the original performance space, but it must have caused the spectators to gasp, especially as the mechana swung Medea's chariot out of sight away 'to Athens'.

Despite the distance between them and the implicit disparity of status, Medea and Jason are both cruelly injured and soon begin to hurl recriminations at each other like two ordinary human beings. This could become a second **agon** for them although it never develops into a formal debate – dramatically it is far too late to argue the issue again and raw feelings dominate. The audience endure the heart-breaking sight of the children's bodies while we hear Jason and Medea arguing about parenthood with intense hatred in the **stichomythia**.

How will the audience respond to Jason's expression of regret that he ever brought her from 'a barbarous land to a home in Greece' (p.85)? It might have made the original Athenian audience uncomfortable to hear the concept of civilisation, with which they identified, used like a weapon. Jason's words suddenly sound spiteful, unjust, certainly ungrateful, and altogether too petty for such a terrible occasion. They contrast with Medea's tone in her long speech, where she acts and speaks with a godlike authority. Here she describes how she will have the children buried in the 'sanctuary of Hera of the Cape' and how she will institute 'a solemn festival with ritual observances' in Corinth 'to atone for this impious bloodshed' (p.86). She then foretells Jason's death aboard his ship, the *Argo*: he will 'meet a coward's end, struck on the head by part of your *Argo*, so witnessing a bitter end to marrying me' (p.86).

What does Euripides actually show us at the end? Jason and Medea both call on the gods to curse each other, but they have both cursed themselves already through their actions. Medea's triumph is bought at the high price of her sons' murders and her own peace of mind. Nonetheless, she flies away to a new homeland at last, leaving Jason, the oath-breaker, to contemplate the wreck of all his plans for posterity. Why do they recapitulate grievances against one another yet again at the end, other than to leave us with the perplexing sense that either both or neither of them are justified in their own terms?

Key point

Euripides deliberately makes it difficult for the audience to assign blame in a simplistic way. It is only possible to take sides easily ('love Medea, hate Jason') if we feel no compassion for the characters and if we haven't paid attention to their points of view. The last stages of the play keep readjusting the emotional balance, too. The play ends by handing all the moral issues back to the audience to think about.

20. Exodus (p.87)

Summary: *The Chorus leave the orchestra space with a neutral speech that closes the play.*

Theme cue: divine justice?

The Chorus of Corinthian women offer no more guidance. Their final speech may sound inadequate as a concluding message to the audience, more like a bemused shrugging of the shoulders than the key to interpretation everyone was hoping for. Who knows what to expect of the gods? Mikalson points out that Euripides 'often closed his plays' with these Choric lines (Mikalson 1991, p.236).

CHARACTERS & RELATIONSHIPS

In the detailed analysis above I have stressed how and why main characters – Medea, Creon, Jason and Aegeus – interact with each other in the episodes; what purpose is served by the secondary characters – Nurse, Tutor, Messenger – and how the Chorus interacts thematically with material in episodes, reflecting or challenging potential audience responses. Below are further cues to guide you in your character studies.

Medea

Key quote

'... Medea, poor lady, dishonoured ...' (Nurse, p.51)

'Watch out for that savage temperament of hers ...' (Nurse, p.53)

'... wrong a woman in love and nothing on earth has a heart more murderous.' (p.57)

'... I shall kill my own children; no one shall take them from me.' (p.71)

Euripides seems to be on Medea's side in this play, we might argue, because he lets her fly away safely at the end to the next stage of her eventful life. Euripides here is concentrating on a single critical moment in a famous relationship. He explores what it is that motivates people to love and then hate each other with great intensity, building inevitably to the tragic outcome.

Medea bitterly appreciates how love for Jason has brought her exile and infamy. But he is also the father of her two children, whom she loves. She does not kill them without doing violence to her own psyche. Given these facts, Medea's tragic equation is understandable, even if we can't condone the end result.

Speaking as a woman, Medea articulates her feelings on jealousy, frustration, childbirth, domestic isolation, bodily submission to a controlling man, and other subjects. What would certainly have confronted the original audience in 431 BC strikes a contemporary audience as legitimate and painfully frank biographical detail. Central to her concerns in life, especially for security, is respect for promises given and it is in this key area that Jason has failed her. Everything else follows from that fact in Euripides' characterisation.

Creon

Key quotes

'Better for me to be hateful now in your eyes than to be talked round by you and regret it bitterly in future.' (p.58)

'I am no tyrant in my heart but a king ...' (p.60)

There are two keys to Creon's character in this play and they are both weaknesses stemming from his family feeling. The first is panic. Because he moves aggressively against Medea to protect his child Glauce, he actually stimulates Medea to think seriously about revenge. The Messenger later describes how Creon in a panic of emotions throws himself on Glauce as she dies, thus infecting himself with the fatal poison. Secondly, despite his bluster, Creon the father is susceptible to Medea's appeals for her children: he relents, giving her the one day's grace she needs to execute her destructive plan. Creon's love is protective but short-sighted in that he chooses the worst strategy to keep Glauce safe when he banishes Medea.

Jason

Key quotes

'... I have not disowned my family and here I am ... looking to your future, my lady, to prevent your being driven out together with our children, either penniless or in need of anything else ...' (p.62)

'You may feel hatred for me, but I could never wish you anything but good.' (p.62)

Once the hero of the Argonauts' expedition, and Medea's lover, Jason is presented as the 'reasonable' man making plans for a settled life in Corinth, through a prudent marriage to the king's daughter. His dismissal of Medea's arguments against him in the **agon** are shown to be indefensible for several reasons, chief of which is that he has betrayed the woman to whom he swore a sacred binding oath, even though the oath itself was not equivalent to legitimate marriage. It's difficult for us to imagine how Jason's character was read by the original audience because, while most of his comments about women and children repel us now, his speeches reflect Athenian views in Euripides' time. Perhaps Euripides was deliberately challenging his audience to start thinking.

Aegeus

Key quote

'... Aegeus, you have a noble heart.' (Chorus-Leader, p.71)

Aegeus, as an honourable man, offers Medea protection in Athens partly out of genuine kindness and respect for Medea, and partly out of self-interest because she can cure his sterility. He is certainly not afraid to be bound by an unbreakable oath; on the contrary, he considers it to be a useful insurance policy if he is ever challenged about sheltering Medea. As far as we are aware, he keeps his word to her.

Euripides was courting unpopularity when he chose to characterise a founding father of the Athenian state as sterile. He then compounded the insult to Athens by underlining Medea's part in Aegeus' cure and her subsequent status as queen of Athens, and mother to a son by Aegeus.

The Nurse

Key quote

'... a good slave's heart shares the pain.' (p.52)

The Nurse is an old woman, loyal to Medea but conservative and cautious. She wants a quiet life without trouble. Hence she expresses views that the audience will recognise as correct and sensible: women ought to be obedient in marriage, and people should try to avoid exile. Her idea is to live without the trauma that she knows afflicts the rich and famous.

One of her central functions in the play is to stir the audience's initial feelings of sympathy and pity for Medea and activate audience fears for the vulnerable children. The poetic comment on music and tragedy (p.55) is the Nurse's last speech in the play, a rare flash of insight. Afterwards she is a silent witness and a messenger only.

Tutor

This old man expresses homely practical advice about making the best of life, which is inevitably unsatisfactory in his experience, a point of view the audience might well share. He accompanies the children with Jason to Creon's palace and acts as a preliminary 'messenger', innocently bringing what he thinks is good news to Medea about Glauce's reception of gifts and the children. We know that the Tutor is habitually closer to the children than the Nurse because Medea orders him to prepare 'their daily food' (p.77). Nevertheless, the audience should be unsettled because he is less sensitive than the Nurse to the danger they are in. He also fatally misreads Medea's tears (p.77) as grief for her own fate rather than the children's.

Chorus

The Chorus of Corinthian women represent at first the voice of the city in which Medea is identified as the outsider. They strongly condemn Jason's oath-breaking, repeating their disapproval several times. Even though they are identified initially as Corinthians, they are not consistently in character. After the Messenger's speech, for example, their comment is about the way Heaven delivers justice to Jason, not about the tragedy that has befallen the Corinthian king and princess.

The Chorus speak as one collective voice about the power of life-shaping invisible forces like Duty and Justice, the seriousness of oaths taken in the names of gods, problems associated with love, with children and with the workings of Fate in human plans. It's important to recognise that they do more than just act as a commentator on the action. The Chorus speak as though they have feelings and thoughts, too. Sometimes they take sides and sway audience opinion; at other times the audience might take issue with a view they express. For example, the sombre ode about children (pp.78–9) explores a whole attitude to life, including the right of women to speak out, rather than simply reflecting on Medea's immediate problems as a mother – although that is part of what they are doing, too.

Messenger

The messenger has a minor but important role because he presents an eyewitness account of events happening 'offstage'. Euripides sketches a few humanising emotional characteristics for the man who, like the Nurse and the Tutor, is also a slave but has an interest in what will happen to Jason and Medea, his masters. The speech has an 'I was there' immediacy.

Children

Medea's sons are mute 'extras' onstage. Their voices behind the skene (p.83) might have been made by one of the adult actors offstage at that moment, or by the young boys themselves. Euripides needs to include the boys as physical presences onstage because they focus audience concerns on the unbelievable horror of Medea's act towards them. Euripides winds up the tension carefully. Medea sends them indoors once, we see them disappear through the skene door – and they come out safely. Medea sends them to Creon's palace with fatal gifts in their innocent hands – and they come home safely. Medea sends them indoors finally and they go through the skene door – moments later she follows them offstage – and we know they are going to die.

THEMES, IDEAS & VALUES

Conflict

The dominant theme of *Medea* is conflict. In particular, *Medea* considers the conflict experienced between people who come from different backgrounds and have different ways of looking at life. It explores how such people:

- **identify** themselves in relation to country, society, family and gender
- **relate** to each other and to the unseen gods
- **balance** reason and emotion, the head with the heart.

From this basis, we can locate the following important related themes, each with a cluster of issues worth tracing through the play. Make notes on each one, with page references, and see if you can discover more issues to add to each list.

Betrayal

Key quotes

'... where love was once deepest a cancer spreads.' (Nurse, p.51)

'The man who was the world to me ... has proved to be the foulest of traitors, my own husband!' (Medea, p.56)

'I betrayed my own father, my own family to come here with you ... and yet you have betrayed me ...' (Medea, p.63)

Betrayal is associated with issues of broken trust, loss of self-worth, guilt, hatred, regret, desire for revenge, contrasting loyalty and disloyalty and the seriousness of oaths.

Being betrayed by someone we trust completely is one of the worst experiences we can ever have in life and it takes a long time to recover.

Suddenly we doubt whether we can ever trust anyone again and we become suspicious of other people's kindness, wondering what they are really after – they can't really want to help, can they? Betrayal may lead to feelings of being worthless – 'I must be awful if I got dumped like that', of guilt and self-blame – 'It must be my fault, I must have done something awful to deserve it', together with panic – 'I'm on my own, no-one's there to help me', accompanied by deep sadness and grief – 'Life isn't worth living any more'.

This is the catastrophe Medea is experiencing at the beginning of the play as the Nurse describes it (Sections 1, 2 and 3) and as you hear from her cries, before you see her onstage (Section 4). She seems to be blaming herself for causing her own ruin but this may be a ploy to fool Creon, whom she hates for banishing her (Section 6).

Other strong feelings that come with betrayal (particularly when it occurs within a marriage or romantic relationship) are directed outwards, towards the betrayer. We may hate the person we loved passionately a few days before if he or she betrays us, especially if we've been replaced by a new partner, whom we also hate, even though we don't know them at all. Along with hatred may come feelings of intense regret for ever loving that person in the first place – 'What on earth did I see in them? How could I have allowed myself to ...' – and a desire for revenge.

Medea experiences both hatred and regret. Because she did terrible things to her own family and homeland in order to be with Jason (Sections 4 and 5), she has a deep nagging guilt, which she has been able to justify to herself only as long as Jason is her lover. Jason has been disloyal to Medea after she staked her whole future on him. She demonstrated her loyalty to him by committing acts of violence to help him succeed. In her view, he has violated her trust, her friendship and their sexual relationship.

'What was it all for?' is the feeling that haunts someone who abandoned security for someone who made a promise, then broke it. Most serious to Medea's way of thinking is that Jason has dishonoured a sacred oath (Sections 4, 8 and 9).

In order to exact her revenge, however, Medea turns into a betrayer. She deliberately misleads Creon (Section 6) and Jason, as well as Glauce, the Tutor and the children (Sections 12 and 17). Whatever kind of positive response we might have had to her earlier in the play is now complicated. But we also cannot forget her **psychomachia** (Section 15), the high point of her conflict in relation to betrayal.

Q Consider Medea as the betrayed and the betrayer. Do you think her responses to Jason's betrayal are understandable? Justified?

Q What does Medea's behaviour as a partly divine figure suggest about the power and behaviour of gods and fate?

Exile

Key quotes

'... in the case of one who has made his home in a strange city, he must take pains not to alienate the community he has joined.' (Medea, p.56)

'... many are the troubles that exile carries in its wake.' (Jason, p.62)

'To be denied one's native land is a misery beyond all others.' (Chorus, p.67)

Exile is associated with issues of identity and belonging; a feeling for home and security; the sense of belonging versus the threat of being an outcast; feeling isolated, friendless, abandoned. It involves alienation, a life disrupted and being identified negatively as 'other'.

Medea speaks to us with special poignancy, I think, because issues about belonging and 'place' affect so many of us directly, or through family histories. Being in exile means being separated from our roots, from the familiar environment and community structure in which we grew up. It could mean having to lose our own language and struggling to learn a new one, or having to change dress and eating habits, or religious practices, even leaving behind sacred objects, places and 'old gods'. The depth of isolation and alienation that all of this brings about is not easy to fathom, for anyone who has not experienced it. Everything is different. Added to this trauma is the likelihood of being shunned for looking, sounding, smelling and being *different*, and therefore being feared and misunderstood.

This theme, with its issues, focuses on Medea's plight especially, and the disruptive pattern of her life. Recurrent sea imagery underlines the feeling of being on the move, always seeking a safe harbour, 'a haven … in heavy seas' (p.71). Creon fears Medea specifically as a foreign woman with magic arts (Section 6), something unknown in civilised Corinth. The Chorus understand sufficiently to imagine themselves in Medea's position (Section 9). When considered in the context of the theme of exile, Aegeus' offer of sanctuary in Athens and the depth of Medea's gratitude (Section 10) become more significant.

Remember that Jason, too, has been a wanderer. Part of his motivation for marrying Glauce is to establish himself somewhere, in one place, and identify himself as a member of a community through alliance with the royal family (Section 8). A nomadic life with Medea and his two stateless sons cannot give Jason the security he must feel to identify himself as a citizen of a civilised place.

Q Look at how and why Medea is exiled from her own people and the part this plays in her fury at Jason's betrayal of her.

Reason and passion

Key quotes

'… my passion is master of my reason …' (Medea, p.78)

'Any man of good sense should never have his children taught to be unusually clever … they invite the envy and hostility of their fellow citizens.' (Medea, p.58)

'A woman who is hot-tempered, and likewise a man, is easier to guard against than one who is clever and controls her tongue.' (Creon, pp.58–9)

'May I know the blessing of a heart that is not passion's slave …' (Chorus, p.67)

Reason and passion are associated with issues related to expressing emotions or exercising self-control. These include rational argument versus angry passionate expression, using a mask of rationality to manipulate or conceal feelings and balancing head and heart. Passion can erupt into loss of control and madness and danger in personality.

Why should there be a perceived division between reason and passion? Arguments about whether self-control is preferable to emotional expression, and under what circumstances, are part of an ancient conflict which is still unresolved. As children we may be allowed to express emotions freely but as we 'grow up' (as in 'why don't you grow up?') we get the idea that adult behaviour should be 'rational', by which we mean that words and actions should be governed by thought. Using phrases like, 'Don't get emotional' or 'Let's be rational about this' is one way adults curb each other's outbreaks of passion. Only in highly controlled and approved social circumstances of limited duration, like a funeral or a football match, are strong emotions usually demonstrated in public.

Medea terrifies the Nurse, the Tutor, the Chorus and Creon (Sections 1, 2, 5 and 6) because she is violently expressive about her suffering and injury. However, the self-control she is capable of exercising (Sections 5, 6, 7, 12 and at the end) surprises the audience who have been anticipating a passionate outburst. Medea knows how to control and direct her passionate energy.

'Nothing in excess' was the philosophical ground-rule of civilised life in democratic Athens. Balanced though this idea might sound, 'excess' probably referred more to over-expression of passion than over-application of the thinking process, since self-control, sophrosyne, was the valued ideal for an individual citizen. As we know, it is possible to use reasoning power emotionally and for specific emotional ends, to plead a special case, to persuade someone, to manipulate their perceptions, or to justify shady acts, which we call 'rationalising', a word that has negative connotations. This is how both Medea – planning 'honeyed words' to trick Jason (p.71) – and Jason – justifying his changed loyalties by stressing how important it is to have governed emotions (Section 12) – use reason to serve their own ends.

Despite considerable evidence to the contrary in our everyday experiences, the view that there is a fundamental divide between reason and passion, between the head and the heart, still holds. *Medea* explores the way both head and heart define a human being and shape human relationships, illustrating the terrible consequences when one is dominant, and the other mistrusted or devalued.

Q Trace Medea's moves from passion to reason but also note how she does use reasoning power emotionally and for specific ends. Do you think Medea is controlled by her passion, or, given her circumstances, that she is reasonable in being so passionate?

Justice and revenge

Key quotes

'… there is no justice in the eyes of men …' (Medea, p.56)

'… it is my view, however … that you have betrayed your wife and are behaving unjustly …' (Chorus-Leader to Jason, p.65)

Justice and revenge are associated with issues to do with the sacredness of oaths, and with how to deal with acts that pollute sacred bonds of family and the gods. This play also forces us to consider whether passion ever justifies violence.

When people swear solemn oaths, especially if they appeal to gods acknowledged by everyone in that community, they are expected to honour their word. We know that we can make promises 'with our fingers crossed' but that they are not real promises; we give ourselves permission to dishonour them later. Justice is about being just, that is, behaving in a fair and ethical way, according to the law. Who punishes us if we break our word? Do we believe that some divine force is watching and judging our actions? Remember that the Greeks personified Justice in two goddesses, Themis – the right way of doing things, established by law, and Dike – justice, including ideas of punishment and revenge. Greek myths are full of stories about people who incur divine justice: some of the worst punishments are reserved for crimes against family or crimes that violate sacred bonds of hospitality or duty.

Shakespeare's *Macbeth*, also a tragedy, illustrates punishment for violating these bonds, exploring the themes of justice and revenge. Writing in Shakespeare's time, an English lawyer considered that revenge is a kind of 'wild justice', only permissible, perhaps, when the law can do nothing to help the injured party. He goes on to warn that revenge brings its own trauma to the perpetrator, plus the chance of further retribution. One of the great unresolved debates in Greek tragedy revolved around where the gods stood in relation to human activity, particularly as dispensers of justice. Characters might appeal to gods to dispense divine justice for wrongs but, in Euripides' plays at least, the gods are silent. Wrongs are more than likely to go unpunished, except through human acts.

Medea's charge against Jason is that he has broken an oath to her that was sworn to the gods (Section 4). He is therefore doubly guilty and deserving of divine punishment. The Chorus agree (Sections 3 and 5). Contrast Aegeus' willingness to take an oath by the gods, happy to know it will bind him to keep his word and so avoid future potential difficulties (Section 10).

Rather than wait for Zeus to help her, Medea chooses to take up her own revenge, claiming that what she will do is just, since Jason does not respect oaths given to the gods.

Q Trace how Medea develops her plan for revenge (Sections 12, 14, 15 and 19). Two Choric odes reflect on Medea's plan: she claims that tragic necessity impels her to kill her children, but the Chorus worry about the pollution of shedding family blood (Section 11) and weigh up the emotional toll of personal revenge (Section 13).

Parents and children

Key quotes

'... only my children win more love from me than my country.' (Creon, p.59)

'To save my children from exile, I would give my life, not merely gold!' (Medea, p.76)

'... those mortals who have produced children are less fortunate than those who have no experience at all of parenthood.' (Chorus, p.79)

Medea raises many issues associated with parenting: parental feelings and hopes, the significance of the family and the psychological and emotional repercussions when children are destroyed.

For some people, the most shocking aspect of this play is how Medea plans to avenge herself on Jason by deliberately setting out to kill her own sons. Child murderers have been fiercely condemned in the media in recent times.

Medea examines specific issues about parental behaviour towards children. While for most people having children is just something that happens as part of an adult relationship, as with Medea bearing Jason's children, or the way Jason assumes that Glauce will bear his children to be 'brothers' for Medea's sons (p.74), children sometimes take on a significance beyond this. They can embody the hopes of powerful men like Creon (Sections 6 and 17), Aegeus (Section 10) and Jason (Sections 8, 12 and 19), all of whom articulate the significance of establishing and protecting a dynasty through heirs, although Jason asserts he would prefer that he did not need a woman to beget children (p.65). Jason's 'love' for his children is questionable in Medea's view, since he has deserted them. Creon and Jason see their family hopes destroyed; Aegeus is rewarded for helping Medea by being granted a family.

Killing her children to wound Jason certainly has the desired outcome for Medea but she, too, is driven to frenzy by her decision (Sections 11 and 15) and has to take elaborate precautions in burial and cult establishment to avert the consequences of her blood guilt (Section 19).

The Chorus also raise issues on this theme. They worry about Athens accepting a child murderer and Medea's capacity to carry out the act (Section 11), then reflect on the misfortune of having children. Section 16 is almost Brechtian in its effect of making 'conventional' voices take up an argument so contrary to the social norm. Finally, they react to the moment of killing and ponder its consequences by reminding the audience of the mythic example of Ino, another child killer (Section 18).

Q Medea's terrible act of killing her sons is justified in her mind. Ensure that you know her reasons and arguments for this as well as others' positions. What is your considered response to this issue?

Gender antagonism

Key quotes

'Of all creatures that have life and reason we women are the most miserable of specimens!' (Medea, p.56)

'There should have been some other means for mankind to reproduce itself, without the need of a female sex; this would rid the world of all its troubles.' (Jason, p.65)

Gender antagonism is evident in hostility towards the opposite sex. It is also associated with issues of relationships between men and women, arguments expressing women's views and the social and sexual roles of women.

Given that this play was written by an Athenian man, with a male audience in mind, we suppose, and male actors in all the roles, *Medea* raises some very interesting issues about women in society and their relations with men. In all of their comments, Creon and Jason express the conventionally accepted views of an Athenian citizen audience of Euripides' time. That is, they expect women to be respected, if they are respectable; to have a domestic role as wives and mothers; and to be obedient to their menfolk. Jason expresses the extreme of misogynistic intolerance when he claims that if reproduction did not require the existence of women, 'this would rid the world of all its troubles' (p.65). Contrast this attitude to Medea with how Aegeus – the only Athenian character in the play – behaves. Not only is he courteous but he positively respects Medea's intelligence and is grateful for her help.

Views about their lives from the female perspective are presented throughout by the Nurse, the Chorus of Corinthian women and Medea, with a glimpse of Glauce's relationship with Jason from the Messenger's report (Section 17, p.80). Note what I interpret as Medea's *ironic* put-downs of women (p.61 and in Section 12), echoed by the Chorus (Section 16). The Chorus, too, echo Jason's views that women are responsible for wickedness (p.83).

Can women expect to be valued other than as wives and mothers? In her conversation with Creon, Medea seems to regret being 'clever' (Section 6, p.58) but acknowledges Aegeus' compliments with pleasure (Section 10). As a sorceress, she demonstrates that she has extraordinary powers to influence her social situation – which is why she is considered dangerously uncontrollable.

DIFFERENT INTERPRETATIONS

Different interpretations arise from different responses to a text. Over time, a text will give rise to a wide range of responses from its readers, who may come from various social or cultural groups and live in very different places and historical periods. Responses by critics and reviewers can be published in newspapers, journals and books, both online and in print. They can be also expressed in discussions among readers in the media, classrooms, book groups and so on.

While there is no single correct reading or interpretation of a text, it is important to understand that an interpretation is more than a personal opinion – it is the justification of a point of view on the text. To present an interpretation of the text based on your point of view you must use a logical argument and support it with relevant evidence from the text.

The critics' viewpoints

Medea has a long history, both as a literary text and as a script for the stage. Critical responses can be found either as scholarly and academic discussions of the work (including interpretations of the themes and ideas), or in reviews of theatrical performances. Indeed, each theatrical production is an 'interpretation' in and of itself, since the director and company will make decisions throughout the process which emphasise certain elements of the play and particular features of characters. In this way, stage versions will each offer a viewpoint on the narrative. For example, one production might present Medea as a wronged individual whose rational actions are justified, while another might portray her as dangerous, mad and cruel.

Reviews of stage versions of Medea describe her as everything from 'defiant and more than a little deranged' (Mark Fisher in *The Guardian*, reviewing a modernised production in Glasgow in 2013 which starred Rachael Stirling as Medea) to 'chilly, elegant' (Vincent Canby in a

New York Times review of a production nearly two decades earlier, in which Medea was played by Diana Rigg – Stirling's mother!).

Similarly, academic interpretations of the text have varied widely in the centuries since the play was written. Such responses are influenced by the critic's historical context as well as by their individual perspective and background. For example, the ancient Greek philosopher Epictetus describes Medea's murder of her sons as 'an act of a noble spirit' (cited by Hale), while contemporary scholar Stuart Lawrence argues that 'her "morality" turns out to be a rationalization of her vengefulness' (Lawrence 2013, p.4).

The following discussion shows how textual evidence (sometimes even the same quotation or event) can be used to support two contrasting interpretations of the play.

Two interpretations

Interpretation 1

***Medea* portrays a world without kindness.**

The play presents characters who experience great misery at the hands of their friends and loved ones (with little evidence of the gods' intervention). There is barely any compassion shown between individuals. Even when Medea and Aegeus help each other, they do so only to ensure the best outcome for themselves, not because they have a real desire to lessen each other's suffering. Other evidence to support this reading includes:

- Jason betrays his wife, breaking the oaths he has made to her, and causing her pain and grief.
- Creon refuses to relent or show kindness to the wronged Medea, banishing her for his own selfish purposes (and motivated primarily by fear).
- One of Medea's main reasons for killing her children arises from her betrayal by Jason; she says the murders are the means by which she can cause him the most pain (p.72). This shows her inability to forgive, and her willingness to be cruel to the children, her husband and even herself (as she also suffers from the children's deaths).

- Even the Chorus members – representing the world beyond the main characters – are shown to be unkind: when they know Medea is killing her sons, they cannot bring themselves to intervene, asking 'Should I enter the house? Yes, I will save the children from slaughter!' but then ignoring the children's pleas for help, remaining outside to mourn the cruelty of women such as Medea (p.83).

Interpretation 2

***Medea* suggests that humans are flawed and hurt each other even when they intend to protect each other.**

The great suffering throughout *Medea* can be seen to result from poor decisions and people's inability to do the right thing by each other. In this reading, *Medea* portrays a world in which kindness *is* possible, but is rarely shown or expressed.

For example, Jason's initial betrayal was, in his own words, his attempt to be 'a true friend' to Medea and their children (p.64), and to 'provide security' for their family (p.66). However, this (alleged) attempt at kindness did not help Medea in any way; instead, she was, and remains, deeply hurt. Other evidence for this interpretation includes:

- When Medea is murdering her children, the Chorus cry 'Should I enter the house? Yes, I will save the children from slaughter!' Despite their good intentions, they become caught up in a philosophical reflection on the moment and are too late to help (p.83).
- One of Medea's justifications for killing her children is to shield them from shame and poor treatment: 'I will not leave my children to the mockery of my enemies' (p.78). Yet, her attempt to protect them is pitifully flawed: their deaths are surely more hurtful than 'mockery' would have been.
- Creon banishes Medea out of a kindness to his own family – he fears Medea and hopes to protect his daughter. But instead, by exiling Medea he pushes her to a new level of passion and savagery, resulting in not only his daughter's death but ultimately his own.

QUESTIONS & ANSWERS

Essay writing – an overview

An essay on a literary work is a formal and serious piece of writing that presents your point of view on the text, usually in response to a given topic. Your 'point of view' in an essay is your interpretation of the meaning of the text's language, structure, characters, situations and events, supported by detailed analysis of textual evidence.

Analyse – don't summarise

In your essays it is important to avoid simply summarising what happens in a text.

- A **summary** is a description or paraphrase (retelling in different words) of the characters and events. For example: 'Macbeth has a horrifying vision of a dagger dripping with blood before he goes to murder King Duncan.'
- An **analysis** is an explanation of the real meaning or significance that lies 'beneath' the text's words (and images, for a film). For example: 'Macbeth's vision of a bloody dagger shows how deeply uneasy he is about the violent act he is contemplating – as well as his sense that supernatural forces are impelling him to act.'

A limited amount of summary is sometimes necessary to let your reader know which part of the text you wish to discuss. However, always keep this to a minimum and follow it immediately with your analysis of what this part of the text is really telling us.

Plan your essay

Carefully plan your essay so that you have a clear idea of what you are going to say. The plan ensures that your ideas flow logically, that your argument remains consistent and that you stay on the topic. An essay plan should be a list of **brief dot points** – no more than half a page.

- Include your central argument or main contention – a concise statement (usually in a single sentence) of your overall response to the topic. See 'Analysing a sample topic' for guidelines on how to formulate a main contention.
- Write three or four dot points for each paragraph indicating the main idea and evidence/examples from the text. Note that in your essay you will need to *expand* on these points and *analyse* the evidence.

Structure your essay

An essay is a complete, self-contained piece of writing. It has a clear beginning (the introduction), middle (several body paragraphs) and end (the last paragraph or conclusion). It must also have a central argument that runs throughout, linking each paragraph to form a coherent whole.

See examples of introductions and conclusions in the 'Analysing a sample topic' and 'Sample answer' sections.

The introduction establishes your overall response to the topic. It includes your main contention and outlines the main evidence you will refer to in the course of the essay. Write your introduction after you have done a plan and before you write the rest of the essay.

The body paragraphs argue your case – they present evidence from the text and explain how this evidence supports your argument. Each body paragraph needs:

- **a strong topic sentence** (usually the first sentence) that states the main point being made in the paragraph
- **evidence** from the text, including some brief quotations
- **analysis** of the textual evidence explaining its significance and **explanation** of how it supports your argument
- **links back to the topic** in one or more statements, usually towards the end of the paragraph.

Connect the body paragraphs so that your discussion flows smoothly. Use some linking words and phrases like 'similarly' and 'on the other hand', though don't start every paragraph like this. Another strategy is to use a significant word from the last sentence of one paragraph in the first sentence of the next.

Use key terms from the topic – or synonyms for them – throughout, so the relevance of your discussion to the topic is always clear.

The conclusion ties everything together and finishes the essay. It includes strong statements that emphasise your central argument and provide a clear response to the topic.

Avoid simply restating the points made earlier in the essay – this will end on a very flat note and imply that you have run out of ideas and vocabulary. The conclusion is meant to be a logical extension of what you have written, not just a repetition or summary. Writing an effective conclusion can be a challenge. Try using these tips:

- Start by linking back to the final sentence of the second-last paragraph – this helps your writing to 'flow', rather than leaping back to your main contention straight away.
- Use synonyms and expressions with equivalent meanings to vary your vocabulary. This allows you to reinforce your line of argument without being repetitive.
- When planning your essay, think of one or two broad statements or observations about the text's wider meaning. These should be related to the topic and your overall argument. Keep them for the conclusion, since they will give you something 'new' to say but still follow logically from your discussion. The introduction will be focused on the topic, but the conclusion can present a wider view of the text.

Essay topics

1. 'Jason's decisions are based on reason and careful judgement; Medea's decisions are based on passion and selfishness.' Discuss.
2. The Messenger asks Medea, "Are you thinking straight, my lady? Are you sane?" (p.79). What does *Medea* suggest about reason and self-control?

3 'Medea is ultimately careless of family ties, while the men – Creon, Jason and Aegeus – are obsessively concerned with their family interests.' Do you agree?

4 'Euripides has no sympathy with appeals to the gods. He shows that humans choose their own course and then ask for divine sanction to justify themselves.' Discuss.

5 "Ah, the loves of mortal men! What a boundless source of woe!" (Medea, p.59) To what extent does *Medea* show us that love brings pain?

6 Consider some key points of difference between men's and women's experiences of life in this play. Is Euripides a feminist?

7 Discuss the significance of showing Medea's two children onstage as performers.

8 'Medea's actions are justifiable.' Discuss.

9 Comment on the dramatic importance of the minor characters: the Nurse, the Tutor and the Messenger.

10 Discuss the significance of one of the Choric odes in context.

Analysing a sample topic

The Messenger asks Medea, "Are you thinking straight, my lady? Are you sane?" What does *Medea* suggest about reason and self-control?

Use the following notes and prompt questions to brainstorm this topic.

- When does the Messenger say this? After he's brought bad news, which Medea says is 'welcome'. What horrifies him – that she calls him her 'benefactor', that is, a person who does good to somebody in need?
- Next consider her reply: 'I … have a reply I might make to what you have said'. Although to the Messenger Medea appears to be behaving unthinkingly, driven by her passions, in fact here she is quite in control of her emotions, thoughts and words. This suggests that one's sanity and reason might be a subjective state: perceived differently by those on the outside.

- Consider other characters' behaviour in *Medea* which offers evidence on the value of 'sanity'; for example, was Jason 'thinking straight' when he betrayed Medea? What about when he justified his actions to her? What are the implications of characters' 'sane' or 'reasoned' actions? What about those actions that do not appear to be sane or reasoned? What do these forms of textual evidence suggest about reason and self-control? Does the text argue that they are positive qualities? Negative qualities? Somewhere in between?
- Finally, you could think about the meaning of 'sane' more deeply. Refer back to Medea's psychomachia – the terrible struggle she has just had about harming her sons. The Messenger's news now commits her to carry out their murders and it breaks her heart. So, her reply might well conclude with a paradox: yes, I'm thinking straight when I say I'm happy to have killed Glauce – and yet, I'm also *not* sane, because I know I have to finish the revenge on Jason in a minute by killing our children.
- Remember to consider all parts of the question (key words include 'reason' and 'self-control' – though these are similar, discuss *both* carefully), as well as the terms, ideas and context of the quotation.

SAMPLE ANSWER

'Jason's decisions are based on reason and careful judgement; Medea's decisions are based on passion and selfishness.' Discuss.

Jason is portrayed as a man of conventional ambitions. He has been heroic and resourceful in his leadership on the quest for the Golden Fleece, and now has married Glauce, gaining effective rule over Corinth. But, instead of accepting Jason's pragmatic decision, one that could have acted in her children's favour, Medea, still 'transfixed by desire', reacts instinctively and immoderately. The killing of Glauce, Medea's rival for Jason's affection, is understandable, yet her final act goes beyond all reason. She becomes, in Jason's words, an 'abomination' – a 'Tuscan Scylla' – in the eyes of all morally minded Greeks. Medea's actions bespeak unreason, untempered passion: the madness of all-consuming selfishness.

Medea is first encountered plunged into an abyss of hopeless despair: 'Oh, I am wretched, pity me for my sufferings! Oh, if only I could die'. The children's Nurse takes fright, rightly describing Medea's mood as 'savage', and sends the children away. Indeed, Medea's passions do make her savage and will prove dangerous, for the children, for Glauce and Creon, and even for herself. While she acts with little consideration for others' needs or feelings, she recognises in Jason a selfishness which is even more extreme than her own. She sees herself as 'foreign' and powerless to stop Jason, yet her passion strengthens her. As she says quite early to Creon, 'my circumstances at present do not encourage me to offend against kings'. However, Medea can, and does, 'offend' and exact revenge, having nothing to lose in contemplating a dreadful course of action.

Despite acting selfishly and being driven by passion, there is evidence in the text to suggest that Medea is also capable of reason and careful (if misguided) judgement. For example, she makes her plans in great detail, even thinking ahead to potential consequences. She knows she will be unwelcome after committing murders, so she decides to 'delay for just a short while' until she can find a way to ensure her escape. Before carrying out her crimes of passion, she secures a refuge in Athens with Aegeus. This suggests her decisions are sometimes driven by reasoned judgement, as does Creon's accusation that she is 'clever and controls her tongue' rather than being 'hot-tempered'.

Similarly Jason, while he often seems rational and calm, is also flawed in his behaviour. He does make a great play of reasoned and careful judgement in putting aside Medea in favour of Glauce, yet there surely were other motives, as the Chorus allude to when they suggest he has acted 'unjustly'. Power is uppermost in his mind and speech. Jason, middle-aged and now quite unadventurous, has seen how he can build upon his fading reputation and ingratiate himself with Creon. For Jason, too, a kind of passion (perhaps for power rather than for the love of others) is a motivating factor in his decisions. So, even as he tries to win over Medea with vague promises for herself and for the boys' future, every word he utters rings false. He is unreasoned and hasty in his judgement, and therefore equally as selfish as the betrayed Medea.

Perhaps Euripides wanted merely to reinforce the importance of stable, established relationships between men and women, between those who are dominant and those who are expected to be submissive or servile. But Euripides effectively undermines all expectations and presents the audience with situations and actions that cause a high degree of discomfort, and even horror. He poses more problems for his audience than can be answered by reference to conventional standards, and in this lies the enduring fascination of the play. The lines between reason and passion, between the rational and the irrational, are blurred. Of course, one could admire Jason's pragmatism in making Glauce his wife, but we see what his selfishness costs him, his family and Corinth. On the other hand, we can recognise the justice of Medea's claim, but be appalled by the outcome of her loss of control, her selfishness. Jason's and Medea's quarrels and actions suggest that there is no way in which the ancient Greek values of order and proportion – let alone justice – can be achieved, when human passions stand in the way of good judgement.

REFERENCES & READING

The text

Euripides 2003, *Medea and Other Plays*, trans. John Davie, Penguin, London.

Further reading

Easterling, PE (ed.) 1997, *The Cambridge Companion to Greek Tragedy*, Cambridge University Press, Cambridge.

In particular, see **Chapter 4, 'The pictorial record'** by Oliver Taplin, for two paintings of Medea in her dragon-drawn chariot, pp.78–9; and **Chapter 11, 'Tragedy in performance: nineteenth and twentieth-century productions', by Fiona Macintosh**. See especially pp.312–21, giving descriptions of Medea in several productions, including two in 1986: an all-male, kabuki-inspired production directed by Yukio Ninagawa for the 1986 Edinburgh Festival, then, in London, the Vellacott translation with Madhur Jaffrey as Medea.

Hale, Steven, 'Epictetus: From The Discourses', http://facstaff.gpc.edu/~shale/humanities/literature/world_literature/discourses.html

Lawrence, Stuart 2013, *Moral Awareness in Greek Tragedy*, Oxford University Press, Oxford.

Leacroft, R and H 1984, *Theatre and Playhouse*, Methuen, London.

See pp.6–15 for conjectural reconstructions of the Theatre of Dionysos Eleutherios in Athens.

Lloyd, M 1992, *The Agon in Euripides*, Oxford University Press, Oxford.

Mikalson, JD 1991, *Honor Thy Gods. Popular Religion in Greek Tragedy*, University of North Carolina Press, Chapel Hill and London.

Pickard-Cambridge, A 1988, *Dramatic Festivals of Athens*, revised J Gould and DM Lewis, 2nd edn., Clarendon Press, Oxford.

Provides thorough coverage of all known information about this period of theatre.

Rehm, Rush 1992, *Greek Tragic Theatre*, Routledge, London and New York.

Both Easterling and Rehm have extensive and useful bibliographies.

Stanford, WB 1983, *Greek Tragedy and the Emotions*, Routledge & Kegan Paul, London.

Vellacott, P 1975, *Ironic Drama: A Study of Euripides' Method and Meaning*, Cambridge University Press, Cambridge.

Website

The Medea Homepage, http://facstaff.gpc.edu/~shale/humanities/literature/world_literature/medea.html

Contains useful links to critical *Medea* sites.

Film

Medea 1970, dir. Pasolini, San Marco, Les Films Number One (co-production: Paris), Janus Film und Fernsehen. Starring Maria Callas.

The film (starring the famous Greek opera singer) brings out the 'supernatural' quality of Glauce's destruction, as well as showing how Medea's gifts work psychologically to drive Glauce crazy. In the film version, we see the events twice, first as Medea 'visualises' the bride's death in flames and secondly as it happens in reality, where she just seems to run mad and throw herself over the cliff. Compare, also, how play and film treat Medea's killing of the boys. In Euripides' play there is noise, screaming, terror, cries for help. In the film, Medea's weary tenderness towards her boys is stressed – there is no struggle, they are killed gently in her arms.

Reviews

Canby, Vincent 1994, 'SUNDAY VIEW; Diana Rigg Is A Chilly, Elegant Medea', *The New York Times*, 17 April, http://www.nytimes.com/1994/04/17/theater/sunday-view-diana-rigg-is-a-chilly-elegant-medea.html

Fisher, Mark 2012, '*Medea* – review', *The Guardian*, 3 October, http://www.theguardian.com/stage/2012/oct/03/medea-review

Music

Dance: Samuel Barber, the modern American composer, wrote a suite of music on the theme of Medea's revenge for the dancer Martha Graham.

Opera: two powerful operas on the story of Medea are by Charpentier (1693) and Cherubini (1797).

GLOSSARY

Agon: The argument presented between two great opponents in a formally recognised debate pattern. In *Medea*, Medea (the protagonist – the main character) contests issues with Jason (the antagonist). See *Medea*, pp.62–7.

Aphrodite: The goddess of love and beauty who could exercise awesome but unpredictable powers in a person's life. Named after her home on the island of Cyprus, the 'dread Cyprian' (p.67) could spread chaos among civilised communities.

Aulos: The flute player who remained on stage and stood to accompany the Chorus songs (odes).

Choric ode: A formal verse sung by the Chorus, accompanied by the flute. See *Medea* pp.61–2; 67; 72–3 and 76 for examples.

Deus ex machina: Literally 'the god from the machine'. A device to sort things out summarily at the end of the play. Medea can be described as a 'deus ex machina' when she appears above the skene in a Sun-chariot drawn by dragons.

Ekkeklema: Wooden trolley used to bring things out from behind the skene; not as important in *Medea* as the mechana – see below.

Episodeion: Dialogue between two characters in which important action occurs. These episodes move the action of the play along and differ from interactions between the Chorus and a main character which develop and reveal character.

Hecate: Queen Hecate, an ancient mysterious goddess with dangerously magical powers, venerated by Athenians. She taught sorcery and was the dark aspect of Artemis, with powers over the moon, the earth and the underworld. She is Medea's 'chosen accomplice' (p.61), invoked in a trance-like prayer.

Helios: Medea claims descent from Helios, the Sun-god – sometimes referred to simply as 'the Sun' (p.61). At the end of the play she escapes in the dragon-drawn chariot of her 'father's father', the Sun (p.84).

Mechana: A crane; an essential piece of equipment on stage used to great effect when Medea rises above the skene as a semi-divine figure.

Monody: An ode for one voice or actor expressing personal lament. Medea's first speech from inside the house is a monody. In other sections where others are listening I have used the term 'solo'.

Orchestra: The area belonging to the Chorus. There is hot debate about the shape of this area and its connection with the skene space, where the actors are usually placed.

Parados: The parade in of the Chorus.

Peripeteia: A sudden reversal of events; a turnaround.

Proem: A preface to a main speech that signals to the audience the kind of speech that will follow. Medea, in her introduction to her long reply to Jason, insults him, then comments self-reflexively on her inability to describe him as harshly as she would like: 'my tongue can utter no worse abuse against your spinelessness' (p.62).

Prologos: Prologue; the lines introducing the whole play.

Protagonist: Main actor/character in a play; a term now used for novels as well. Clearly Medea is the protagonist.

Psychomachia: A 'battle in the soul'. This is an intense inner conflict between good and evil choices that tears a person apart psychologically. Medea's psychomachia is in Section 15, pp.77–8.

Skene: Originally a hut or tent as a changing room behind the orchestra space for actors to make entrances and exits. Then came a wooden back wall with a central door, which is what *Medea* seems to be using. Stone walls and side structures came after Euripides' time. 'Scene' comes from skene.

Sophrosyne: Self-control, the valued ideal for an individual Athenian citizen.

Stichomythia: A pattern of dialogue where characters exchange single lines in a rapid sequence, to increase tension in an argument. See Creon and Medea in Section 6, p.59 when Medea is trying to gain extra time; and Jason and Medea's intense argument about parenthood in the stichomythia in Section 19, pp.85–7 (though note that Medea also has a longer speech within this section, on p.86).

Sun-god: See Helios in this glossary.